After
"I Believe"

After "I Believe"

Experiencing Authentic Christian Living

Mark D. Roberts

Baker Books

A Division of Baker Book House Co
Grand Rapids, Michigan 49516

Published in association with Yates & Yates, LLP, Literary Agents, Orange, California.

Published by Baker Books
a division of Baker Book House Company
P.O. Box 6287, Grand Rapids, MI 49516-6287

Printed in the United States of America

Library of Congress Cataloging-in-Publication Data

Roberts, Mark D.
    After "I believe" : experiencing authentic Christian living /
Mark D. Roberts.
       p. cm.
    Includes bibliographical references.
    ISBN 0-8010-6389-2 (pbk.)
    1. Christian life—Presbyterian authors. I. Title.
BV4501.3 .R63 2002
248.4—dc21   2001058246

For current information about all releases from Baker Book House, visit our web site:
http://www.bakerbooks.com

I dedicate this book to my wife, Linda,
my partner in Christian living.
How thankful I am for the intimate fellowship
we share together.

Contents

Preface

"Lisa, is there any reason you cannot pray right now to receive Jesus as your Lord and Savior?" I asked expectantly. Because we had spent the previous hour talking about Lisa's desire to know God personally, I was pretty certain of her answer.[1]

"No, I don't think there is," she replied. "I know I want Jesus in my life."

"Well, we ought to pray," I said. "I'll start and then you pray after I'm finished. Use your own words, praying in a way that feels comfortable to you. Tell Jesus why you need him and that you are putting your trust in him. Commit your life to him, and he will give you the gift of eternal life."

So we prayed. And right there, in my office at Irvine Presbyterian Church, a miracle occurred. A young woman entered into an eternal relationship with the living God. Her sins were forgiven. Her heart was refreshed. She began a new life of intimate fellowship with a God who had loved her even before the foundation of the world.

I had the privilege of witnessing this miracle. It's one of the greatest perks of being a pastor. There's not much in life that beats the joy of seeing a person come to faith in Jesus Christ.

Yet, as I rejoiced with Lisa in her newfound Christian faith, my mind turned to the next step. How could I help this brand-new Christian experience the fullness of the life she had just entered? How could I help her "grow in the grace and knowledge of our Lord and Savior Jesus Christ" (2 Peter 3:18 NIV)? Becoming a Christian is the most important experience of life, but it's not the end of God's work in us. It's just the beginning of a lifelong process. Trusting in Jesus opens the door to a new adventure—walking each day with God.

Sometimes, however, people get stuck right at the start of this journey. They think that believing in Jesus is all there is to being a Christian, or that they must go on living just as they always have until they die and go to heaven. This is rather like a man and woman who participate in a wedding, committing themselves to each other yet never actually sharing life with each other. They'd be married but miss all the joys of marriage.

When I have the privilege of leading folks to faith in Christ, I explore with them the joy, the growth, and the fulfillment that come bundled with this new way of living. I talk with them about what it means to experience a meaningful relationship with God each day. We discuss how to pray, how to read the Bible, and how to live for God in the world. I explain the importance of Christian community. But often, as we come to the close of our conversation, I feel frustrated, knowing that I have barely scratched the surface of Christian living. There is so much more I want these new believers to understand so that they might live abundantly as members of God's family.

This book lays out the essential aspects of abundant Christian living. In searching Scripture, I have found the idea of *intimate fellowship* to be a hub around which the multiple aspects of the Christian life rotate with balance and beauty. While I acknowledge there are other metaphors for Christian living in the Bible—pilgrimage, discipleship, abiding, and obedience, for example—the concept of intimate fellowship in particular has helped me, and, I hope, will help you understand what the Christian life is all about.

Although not all the ideas presented here are fully my own, most of them reflect God's own ideas as revealed in Scripture. Additionally, my writing is an outgrowth of hundreds of relationships with other Christians, my anonymous coauthors, if you will. As you read, you'll find explicit references to my years as a youth at Hollywood Presbyterian Church, to my friendships while a student at Harvard, to my pastoral work at Hollywood Presbyterian, to interactions with my seminary students, to experiences with my family, and to my current faith community, Irvine Presbyterian Church, where I am blessed to serve as senior pastor. Apart from the influence of godly people in all of these segments of my life, I would not be able to write this book. Perhaps more than anything else, this book is an extension of my pastoral ministry for the past seventeen years.

This book reflects, beyond all other relationships, my own intimate fellowship with God. Whatever intimacy I have with the Lord is not a matter of my own doing, however; it is a precious gift that has come to me through God's grace, given in Christ, and renewed daily by the Holy Spirit. If you get anything else from this book, I hope you'll learn that the Christian life is not something you produce by your efforts but something you receive as a gift from God.

In offering this book to you, I feel as if I'm giving you a marvelous present. If you unwrap and use this present, you'll experience a fullness of life that you might never have known before. But this gift really isn't from me. I'm just the guy who put it in a box and wrapped it up for you. The Christian life is God's gift to you because he loves you. The God of the universe seeks intimate fellowship with you. He wants to bless you through intimate fellowship with his people. I pray that this book will help you live daily in that life-transforming fellowship. That's what authentic Christian living is all about.

Mark D. Roberts

Acknowledgments

I wish to thank the following people for their help with this book:

Members of Irvine Presbyterian Church, whose response to my preaching has helped me shape this material and who provided me with a sabbatical during which I was able to write this book.

The members of Solana Beach Presbyterian Church and Memorial Drive Presbyterian Church (Houston) who allowed me to develop this material as a speaker for their retreats and whose feedback helped me to sharpen my insights.

Buddy Owens, Hugh Hewitt, and Tod Bolsinger for reading portions of the manuscript and for offering helpful suggestions.

Sealy Yates, my literary agent, for his wisdom and encouragement and for helping me to get this book published.

Don Stephenson, director of publications at Baker Book House, for his vision for and commitment to this book.

Sharon Van Houten, editor at Baker, for her friendly expertise in guiding my manuscript through the editing process.

My family, Linda, Nathan, and Kara, for their patience and support during my long hours of writing.

1
What Is the Christian Life?

"I, Mike, take you, Allison. . . . As a gift from God. . . . To be my wedded wife. . . ." With such revered phrases, I lead earnest grooms to commit their lives to their radiant brides. Then I help the brides return the favor.

Often I'm caught up in the supreme sentiment of a wedding. But, I must confess, there are times when, observing a youthful couple as they gaze adoringly into each other's eyes, I want to shout, "Do you really know what you're getting into?"

Let me reassure you. I don't actually holler during wedding ceremonies. Besides, I don't really need to ask that question because I know the answer already. Do the bride and groom really know what they're getting into? Of course not. Nobody actually knows what marriage is all about before experiencing the unexpected joys and unforeseen sorrows of married life.

Yet those whom I marry have previously satisfied me with their rudimentary knowledge of marriage. In premarital counseling, I always ask couples, "What is marriage?" Answers vary, but they usually reflect several basic perspectives:

Marriage is a friendship that lasts for a lifetime.
Marriage is a business partnership.
Marriage is a means to leave my own family and make a fresh start.
Marriage is a gift from God.

Each of these answers captures a part of what marriage is all about. But each is also less than adequate, in my opinion.

If a couple begins marriage with an inadequate sense of marriage, they threaten the health and longevity of their relationship. For example, marriage is indeed like a business partnership in many ways. But if a spouse sees marriage *primarily* as a business arrangement, problems ensue when the cost-benefit ratio of the relationship falls below an acceptable range. What if a wife believes she is contributing more to the marriage than her husband and is receiving less benefit than her investment merits? If she views marriage simply as a business venture, she has a convincing reason to terminate the marriage partnership.

If, in contrast, two people see marriage as a divinely sealed, lifelong covenant between a man and a woman, they will form a solid foundation for a lasting, fruitful marriage. If they hold on to this vision during the inescapable frustrations of married life, they will have a much better chance of growing through conflict to enjoy the abundant blessings of wedded life. Having a correct understanding of marriage does not guarantee a successful marriage, but it certainly gets newlyweds headed in the right direction.

As with marriage, so it is with the Christian life. How we understand Christian living will impact the health and longevity of our relationship with God. The closer we come to seeing the Christian life accurately, the more likely we will be to thrive as Christians. Yet many of us have only the foggiest notion of Christian living.

When we first became Christians, most of us had almost no conception of the Christian life. By God's Spirit at work in us, we recognized how much we had messed up our lives by rejecting God's will for us. We perceived that a vast chasm separated us from God, and we realized that we could not bridge that gap by ourselves. We needed serious help, God's help, to clean up our lives and to get right with him. Then we heard the good news of what God had done for us in Jesus, who took upon himself our separation from God so that we could know God intimately, just as Jesus himself does (2 Cor. 5:21). All we had to do was acknowledge that our sin had corrupted our relationship with God and put our trust in Jesus to save us (Rom. 3:21–26). As we trusted in him, in his death on the cross for us, we were reborn. We received new life from God above, the best sort of life there is, what the Bible calls "eternal life" (John 3:1–16). From that moment on, we had the chance to live in a completely different way, relying on God's goodness, following God's directives, and enjoying God's presence.

Just as newborn infants have little idea of what life will be like, so it is for most of us who, through faith in Jesus, are reborn as spiritual babies. A few people trust their lives to Christ after an extensive process of examining Christianity. Most of us, however, begin our Christian journey with little idea of where the road leads or what our form of travel will be. God does not require the spiritual equivalent of premarital counseling before someone enters into a permanent covenant with Jesus Christ. Thus, as we begin to live in this relationship, we may well wonder, "What is the Christian life?"

Basic Ideas about the Christian Life

Like marriage, the Christian life is too complex to be captured fully in one simple statement. Biblical metaphors for the Christian life abound, including: walking (Gal. 5:16; Eph. 4:1, 5:2), athletic competition (1 Cor. 9:24–27; Phil. 3:12–14; Heb. 12:1), citizenship (Phil. 3:20), stewardship (1 Peter 4:10), servanthood (2 Cor. 5:18; Eph. 4:12), and apprenticeship (Matt. 28:19; Luke 14:25–33).

Most Christians, even those who are new to the faith, have some rudimentary idea of the life they have begun. As a pastor, I have listened to scores of people describe their conceptions of Christianity. These notions usually reflect one of four basic ideas of the Christian life. Each of these captures one vital aspect of that life. But each also overlooks integral parts.

Idea #1: The Christian Life Is Reserved for Heaven

The assurance of heaven is one of the most precious possessions of any Christian. A couple of years ago, I sat near the bedside of Helen, a dear woman in my congregation whose body had just about given up after eighty plus years of life. Helen knew that her death was near, and she knew it with joyful confidence. "I'm ready to go," she admitted. "It's time. I want to see Jesus." What could be more reassuring than to know that when we die, we will not so much end life as begin a new, enhanced, everlasting life?

We stand on biblical bedrock when we embrace the hope of heaven: "For God has reserved a priceless inheritance for his children. It is kept in heaven for you, pure and undefiled, beyond the reach of change and decay" (1 Peter 1:4). But blissful existence after death does not fully capture the Christian life. The apostle Paul proclaims that, once we have been saved by grace through faith, we join Christ in heaven right now, in a spiritual sense (Eph. 2:6). Jesus speaks of eternal life, that which we associate with afterlife, as a present and a future reality for those who believe in him (John 5:24). Therefore, the Christian life is not only "pie in the sky when you die," to repeat a hackneyed phrase. Rather, the Heavenly Cook lets us stick our fingers into the batter of heaven while it's being prepared. The Christian life happens not just in the future but right now.

Idea #2: The Christian Life is Feeling Joy and Peace in the Lord

Sometimes new believers discover the present reality of the Christian life right away. Many converts, though certainly not all, tingle with joy in the seconds following their first step of faith. Others find their emotional burdens lifted as they taste "God's peace, which is far more wonderful than the human mind can understand" (Phil. 4:7). This initial blush of emotion might linger for days, refreshed through corporate worship and private devotions. The dynamism of joy, so invigorating, healing, and empowering, can lead us to believe that feeling this joy is the essence of the Christian life.

Indeed, Jesus promises overflowing joy to those who live in him (John 15:11). But we must beware of the tendency to reduce Christianity to feelings alone. The culture in which we live, with its loss of respect for truth, has enthroned feelings as the measure of all things. This emotional orientation to life has infected the Western world, including the church. In some quarters of the church, Jesus has become primarily the one who makes us feel better, not the one who saves us from our sin.

Christian living involves every aspect of our being, including our emotions. We are to love God with all that we are

19

(Mark 12:30). We must not reject the emotional dimension of Christian experience, but we shouldn't condense Christian living to emotions alone.

Idea #3: The Christian Life Is Believing the Right Things about God

According to the New Testament, joy and peace come as we believe in Jesus (Rom. 15:13; 1 Peter 1:8). So, if these emotions do not constitute the core of the Christian life, but are gratifying adjuncts to it, is the Christian life primarily a matter of believing?

The Bible unabashedly proclaims the existence and magnitude of truth. Speaking through the Old Testament prophet Isaiah, God says, "I publicly proclaim bold promises. I do not whisper obscurities in some dark corner so no one can understand what I mean. And I did not tell the people of Israel to ask me for something I did not plan to give. I, the LORD, speak only what is true and right" (Isa. 45:19).

To such a truth-speaking God, the psalmist cries out, "Teach me your ways, O LORD, that I may live according to your truth!" (Ps. 86:11). The New Testament echoes this commitment to truth. Jesus says, "You are truly my disciples if you keep obeying my teachings. And you will know the truth, and the truth will set you free" (John 8:31–32; see also John 14:6; 2 Thess. 2:13; and 1 Tim. 4:3).

We begin the Christian life by believing the "word of truth," the good news of what God has done in Jesus (Eph. 1:13 NRSV). We grow as Christians by "speaking the truth in love" (Eph. 4:15 MDR).[1] Abandoning the basic truth of God endangers both the correctness of our theology and the genuineness of our relationship with God (2 John 1:9).

Christians care about right belief, what theologians call "orthodoxy." Consequently, we find ourselves increasingly alienated from a culture that denies the value or even the possibility of knowing truth. We do not affirm the popular, relativistic slogan, "It doesn't matter what you believe, as long as you believe it." For us it makes all the difference in the world what a person believes. Christians do not have faith in faith but faith in a God who has revealed himself in history, in human experience, in the Bible, and most of all in Jesus.

Yet right belief, as important as it is, does not sum up the whole Christian life. Christian faith is not just "believing that" but "believing in." Not only do we *believe that* Jesus died on the cross, but we also *believe in* him to forgive us. We trust him completely for our salvation. Christian faith is an act of mind and will.

Moreover, true faith must be expressed in action. Jesus said, "Anyone who listens to my teaching and obeys me is wise, like a person who builds a house on solid rock" (Matt. 7:24). So, genuine Christian faith involves *believing* key truths about God, *trusting* Christ personally for salvation, and *putting our belief and trust into action* each day.

Idea #4: The Christian Life Is Doing What God Commands

Throughout the Bible, God cares about what we do. His very first words to human beings tell us to do something: "Be fruitful, and multiply" (Gen. 1:28 KJV). Throughout the Old Testament, God continues to give directions to the Israelites, even though he anticipates their inevitable disobedience. The Law and the prophets repeatedly call God's people to live rightly and to avoid sin. This emphasis continues in the New Testament, every book of which contains imperatives, with hundreds coming from the mouth of Jesus himself. The Bible contains a total of 5,953 verbs in the imperative mood. Obviously, God cares about what we do and assumes the right to tell us what to do.

Because the Bible frequently gives directions for living, believers in Jesus have been tempted to turn the Christian life into a to-do list of good works. It makes relating to God so much more predictable if we can enumerate and then check off everything we're required to do. This form of the Christian life can be mastered through astute time management.

Unfortunately for those of us who are drawn to this approach to Christian living, it contradicts the essence of God's work in our lives. We are saved by grace through faith, and we continue to live by grace, not by our best efforts (Eph. 2:8–10; Phil. 2:12–13). If we turn the Christian life into a list of works, we run the risk of nullifying God's grace (Gal. 2:20–21). If a to-do list becomes the essence of our Christian experience, we have lost our center in Christ.

The Christian Life as Intimate Fellowship

The four common ideas outlined above capture crucial components of the Christian life but must not be equated with that life. Each is essential, but none is fully adequate by itself. We must keep looking for a concept broad enough to incorporate the diversity represented by the four common ideas, yet pointed enough to keep Jesus Christ at the center.

We find this concept in the opening chapter of the first letter of John in the New Testament. He begins by talking a lot about life, mentioning, "the Word of life," "life from God" and "eternal life" (1 John 1:1–2). What is this multiform life? Or, better yet, *who* is this life? None other than Jesus Christ. In this identification of Jesus as life we hear echoes of the Gospel of John. There, as the Word of God, Jesus created physical life (John 1:1–4, 10). As the Son of God, he is the source of "eternal life" (John 3:16). As the Good Shepherd, he offers "life in all its fullness" (John 10:10). Jesus is "the way, the truth, and the life," through whom we receive life that conquers death (John 14:6; 11:25–26).

John's equation of Jesus with life is, of course, a figure of speech. It suggests an inseparable connection between him and the divine life, a life John identifies in his letter by the word "fellowship." He is writing about Jesus as eternal life "so that you may have fellowship with us. And our fellowship is with the Father and with his Son, Jesus Christ" (1 John 1:3). If we know Jesus as the Word of life, we will enter into fellowship, the essence of the Christian life.

We often associate fellowship with informal friendliness. Many churches have a "fellowship hall," a place for casual conversation, often complemented with donuts and coffee (the American church's unofficial sacrament). But this casual sense of "fellowship" falls short of the meaning of the Greek word *koinōnia*. This term, translated as "fellowship" in 1 John, means far more than spending time with friendly people. Among Greek speakers in the Roman Empire, *koinōnia* was used for a business partnership. Early Christians used the word for their celebrations of the Lord's Supper, which we call "communion." Marriage could be called "the fellowship of life," and sexual intimacy between spouses could be called *koinōnia*.[2] Clearly, *koinōnia* implies a depth of relationship we don't usually associate with fellowship halls.

It's hard to find an English word that unites the various connotations of *koinōnia*. "Fellowship," "partnership," and "sharing" highlight limited facets of the word's meaning. "Communion" gets much closer, but its religious tone limits the full sense of *koinōnia*. The best translation I can conceive for *koinōnia* uses two English words: "intimate fellowship." God's kind of life involves neither a casual relationship with him over donuts and coffee nor an exclusively religious moment when we "receive communion" in church, but deep fellowship with him at all times and in all places.

What a wonder! The Creator of heaven and earth seeks an intimate relationship with you and me. In our preoccupation with our own search for God, we easily forget that he has been searching for us too. That's the story of the Bible: God's search for humankind, God's effort to reestablish the fellowship between himself and his human creatures that was broken because of sin. Jesus Christ came to save us from sin and death so that we might have a close, lasting relationship with God. As the source of eternal life from God, Jesus welcomes us into *koinōnia* with God—but not with God alone.

Intimate Fellowship with God and God's People

The Christian life is intimate fellowship with God *and God's people*. John writes his letter so that his readers "may have fellowship with us" as well as "with the Father and with his Son" (1 John 1:2–3). The human dimension of *koinōnia* is essential to full Christian fellowship. John reiterates this point in 1 John 1:6–7, where "fellowship with God" is interchangeable with "fellowship with each other." You can't have one without the other because they are inescapably entwined.

The equation of fellowship with God and fellowship with God's people might seem surprising. Isn't the Christian life really about a relationship with God? Isn't the human dimension secondary in significance? If we had to choose between relationship with God and relationship with people, we'd rightly join up with God. But, by making this distinction, we miss the indivisibility of divine and human fellowship that's taught in the Bible. We echo the bias of our culture rather than the revealed word of God.

24

Many popular versions of the Christian life separate that which the Bible holds together so consistently. American individualism has infected our conceptions of Christianity. All that really matters, we are told, is our personal relationship with God. But in biblical perspective, that personal relationship always has corporate implications. We tend to equate personal with private, but the Bible links personal and corporate. A genuine personal relationship with God draws us into genuine personal relationships with people.

Consider the vast sweep of biblical revelation. When God creates a solitary man, God says that it is not good for him to be alone. Therefore, God forms a partner for the man (Genesis 2). God promises to bless Abraham, not all by his lonesome, but by making him the father of a nation and by blessing all the families of the earth through him (Genesis 12). God sets his people free from Egypt not so each Israelite will please God individually but so the congregation of the Israelites will be a "holy nation" together (Exod. 19:6).

Turning to the New Testament, Jesus prayed for those who would one day believe in him, that we might be "perfected into one," even as he was one with his heavenly Father (John 17:22–23). Our Savior died on the cross for our personal salvation and to create one new humanity between formerly divided peoples (Ephesians 2). God's ultimate plan is to "bring everything together" in Christ (Eph. 1:10). In New Testament visions of the afterlife, you will not end up sitting on your own private cloud playing a harp. Rather, you will join a vast heavenly choir, worshipping God in a way that is intensely personal and inescapably corporate (Rev. 7:9–10). That's not all we will do in heaven, but whatever else we do, it won't involve an eternity of playing spiritual solitaire. C. S. Lewis writes that isolation from other people is an essential characteristic of hell, not heaven.[3]

One of the highlights of my life occurred when I was three and a half years old. The spring afternoon was warm as my parents drove across town to finish a process that had taken many long months. When we finally arrived at our destination, I clutched a special teddy bear in one hand while nervously grabbing my mother's fingers in the other. After walking down a long corridor, we stopped at a room. It was sparsely furnished, with a plain wooden crib in the corner. In that crib was a three-month-old baby, my parents' newly adopted son, Gary. My heart raced as I peered at him for the very first time. Dangling the teddy bear before his giant blue eyes, I swelled with pride when Gary smiled at me. This was not just my parents' son. He was my brother.

This remained true throughout our lives, whether we liked it or not. I was still Gary's brother four years after his adoption when I ditched him in the hills above our home and he was lost for hours. Gary was still my brother when he clobbered me on the head with the sharp claw of a hammer just to see what would happen to my head. We were joyfully brothers when we stood together in each other's wedding ceremonies and shared the wonder of holding each other's babies only moments after they were born.

Through the best of times and the worst of times, fellowship with our heavenly Father includes fellowship with his other children. Eternal life is personal life and shared life. It is intimate fellowship with God and, necessarily, with God's people.

Intimate Fellowship and Forgiveness

Once we experience genuine *koinōnia*, we begin to live in a completely different way. Before we had fellowship with God, we lived in spiritual darkness, blinded by our sin (1 John 1:6). But when we entered into *koinōnia* with God, we began to live in the light of divine truth (1 John 1:7). It's impossible, John explains, to have fellowship with God and to continue in a lifestyle of pervasive sin. This does not mean, however, that Christians are sinless, that we always live up to God's standards. When we do fall short, and at times we all do, we don't grit our teeth and strain for greater perfection. Rather, we come before God with an honest admission of our failures: "If we confess our sins to him, he is faithful and just to forgive us and to cleanse us from every wrong" (1 John 1:9).

I am thankful that John mentions sin and forgiveness in his discussion of the Christian life. Even though my theology warns against it, my heart keeps trying to turn the Christian life into a matter of perfect performance. A part of me thinks I will finally live as a Christian if I only try hard enough, if I only do all the right things. Of course, I fall short of this unrealistic goal, both by failing to do many right things and by doing many wrong ones instead. Yet my shortcomings do not separate me from fellowship with God because the blood of Jesus his Son cleanses me from all sin (1 John 1:7). The Christian life is not a matter of perfection, but process, not performance for God, but relationship with a God who offers forgiveness and cleansing through Christ.

Intimate Fellowship Includes the Four Common Ideas about the Christian Life

The concept of intimate fellowship encompasses the four ideas of the Christian life that we examined above. According to *Idea #1,* the Christian life is being in heaven after death. This notion correctly identifies a central hope of our faith, but it puts too much emphasis on postmortem existence, overlooking the present reality of Christian living. When we think of the Christian life as intimate fellowship with God and God's people, we need to understand that this fellowship *begins* the moment we believe in Jesus and *extends* forever. Our *koinōnia* continues beyond death, though we don't have to wait until we die to experience it.

Intimate fellowship also clarifies the biblical sense of heaven. Though Scripture speaks of heaven as a place, it is, most importantly, the experience of God's presence. To be "in heaven" is to be "with God," in the company of God's people (1 Thess. 4:17; Phil. 1:23). For this reason, heaven is a present reality for Christians because we already live with God through Christ (Eph. 2:6) and already have joined the heavenly assembly (Heb. 12:22–23).

Idea #2 pictures the Christian life as feeling joy and peace in the Lord. Although this notion overemphasizes certain emotions, these feelings often proceed from fellowship with Christ and participation in the Christian community. Jesus makes this clear when he says that abiding in him—another way of talking about *koinōnia* —will lead to overflowing joy (John 15:11). Moreover, when in times of worry we share in fellowship with God through prayer, often receiving the supportive prayers of our Christian family, we "will experience God's peace, which is far more wonderful than the human mind can understand" (Phil. 4:7).

Proponents of *Idea #3* highlight the content of faith. For them, the Christian life is believing the right things about God. From John's perspective, right belief leads to genuine *koinōnia* but is not equivalent to it. We must correctly understand who Christ is as the "Word of life" so that we might live in fellowship. *Koinōnia* is not some squishy, subjective relationship with a god of our own formulation. It is a substantive, spiritual relationship with the one God who has revealed himself in Jesus Christ, and with all of those who confess a common faith in Christ.

According to *Idea #4,* Christian living is doing what God commands. As we have seen, true fellowship with God influences our whole life. Our way of walking—our daily behavior—will reflect our relationship with God. We will do what God commands as a result of our intimacy with him, but without separating our good works from their divine source. Because the Christian life is not equivalent to obedience, individual acts of disobedience do not kill that life. Our relationship with God depends on his grace and not on our acts of obedience. Therefore, occasional sin is more like a bad flu than a terminal illness. *Koinōnia* with God heals our sickness and vaccinates us from the virus of sin. Moreover, God places us in fellowship with other Christians so that we might help one another avoid sin and live in a way that pleases God.

Intimate Fellowship and Complete Joy

Failure to engage in fellowship with other Christians won't cause you to lose your salvation or to be hit by a divine lightning bolt. It will, however, keep you from experiencing the fullness of the Christian life, including the joy of the Lord. John writes his first letter not only to promote *koinōnia* but also so that "that *our* joy will be complete" (1 John 1:4, italics added). Although John already has deep fellowship with God, his full joy depends to a great extent on his fellowship with other Christians. Likewise, only if we share together in our relationship with the Lord will our joy be complete.

I learned this lesson last summer when my family and I spent a week in the High Sierra of California. One afternoon I set off by myself for a sightseeing hike to Sherwin Lakes. Without my young children tagging along, nothing interrupted my brisk pace or my alpine meditations. Sheer granite peaks, pungent cedar forests, shimmering alpine lakes—I was just about in heaven. Could I be more joyful than this?

The next day I loaded my backpack with all the provisions for an overnight stay at Sherwin Lakes. This time I didn't go alone. My six-year-old son, Nathan, accompanied me for his first backpacking trip. With him as my partner, I didn't hike as quickly as I had the day before. I didn't see as many sights as I had seen when walking alone or have the leisure to appreciate them without distraction. But my joy was even more supreme than it had been because it was now shared. I could show Nathan the cliffs that had stirred my soul earlier, and he could marvel at them with me: "Dad, they're just hunormous!" Nathan helped me get pleasure from natural trifles I had overlooked just the day before: pine cones, water bugs, and sticks just right for throwing. Every aspect of that trip thrilled my son, whether we were gathering wood for the campfire or bundling up in our sleeping bags. My joy was magnified through fellowship with someone I love.

That's the way it is in the Christian life. I've seen it again and again; koinōnia with God *and* God's people leads to complete joy.

Practical Questions and Answers

1. "How can I begin to experience intimate fellowship with God and God's people?"

Christian koinōnia *comes as a result of trusting Jesus Christ as Savior and Lord. If you have taken this step of faith, you have already begun to experience intimate fellowship. If you have not put your trust in Jesus, I'd urge you to do so.*

2. "I've always thought the Christian life was really a matter of my personal relationship with God, so I haven't ever become a part of a church. How can I find a good church?"

There's no simple answer to this question. First, let me urge you to pray about it. If you faithfully seek the Lord's guidance, he will lead you to a church that is right for you. Second, talk with Christians who live near you. Ask about their churches and consider their recommendations. Most people find a church through friends and family members. Third, check the local Yellow Pages or church web sites. You can find out a lot of information this way.

When you're considering a church, look for evidence that it honors Jesus Christ as Lord and Savior. When you visit the church, see if the worship facilitates intimate fellowship with God, if the preaching is biblically based, and if the people are friendly. Look for programs that might help you grow in full koinōnia. If you have children, be sure to check out ministries for children and youth.

Before you decide to join a church, I encourage you to meet with the pastor. (In a large church, you might meet with one of the associates, not the senior pastor.) Bring a list of the questions that matter most to you. Remember: No church is perfect.

2
Intimate Fellowship and the Holy Spirit

The apostle Paul closes his second letter to the Corinthians with these words: "May the grace of our Lord Jesus Christ, the love of God, and the fellowship of the Holy Spirit be with you all" (2 Cor. 13:13). If we were looking at the Greek original of that last phrase, we'd see the familiar term *koinōnia*. Paul prays for the Christians in Corinth to experience the intimate fellowship of the Holy Spirit.

What is the *koinōnia* of the Spirit? To answer this question, we need some theological background on the nature of the Holy Spirit. It's essential that we do our homework here because the Spirit is indispensable to the Christian life. As we shall see, we experience *koinōnia* with God and with God's people through the presence and activity of the Spirit.

A Growing Understanding of the Holy Spirit

Awareness of the Holy Spirit has grown among Christians during the last several decades. This has occurred, in part, because of the prominence of Pentecostal and so-called "charismatic" expressions of Christianity. *Pentecostal* comes from the Jewish festival of Pentecost, the day when the Holy Spirit was first poured out on Christians. *Charismatic* means "gifted" and focuses on certain "gifts" that can accompany the presence of the Holy Spirit.

Early in the twentieth century, certain Christians had life-changing experiences they attributed to the Holy Spirit. They fashioned a theology of the Christian life in which a "second blessing" of the Spirit was essential for all believers. Pentecostalism was characterized by exuberance in worship and the exercise of spiritual gifts—especially speaking in tongues (or unknown languages)—not generally practiced among Christians.

For years, Pentecostalism remained on the fringes of Christendom. But in the 1960s Pentecostalism began to affect mainstream believers. Both clergy and laypeople had transformational experiences of the Holy Spirit and started to worship in the more expressive style of the Pentecostals. Yet they remained actively involved in their own churches as part of a "charismatic" renewal movement.

Pentecostal expressions of Christianity have moved from the shadows to the limelight. Throughout the world, Pentecostalism is thriving, having become the dominant Christian force in much of the Southern Hemisphere. Still, many Christians, especially those of us in the Northern Hemisphere, aren't exactly sure what to make of the Holy Spirit. The Spirit seems like something mysterious, some power that occasionally whispers in our ears or does miracles. This view is not wholly wrong but actually reflects Jesus' comparison of the Spirit to the unpredictable wind (John 3:8).

Some Christians have filled in the blanks in their understanding of the Holy Spirit with notions floating around in popular culture. The Spirit of God is compared to the "Force" in George Lucas's *Star Wars* saga: an enigmatic, impersonal power that enables people to perform amazing feats. As we become familiar with the Spirit, so we are told, we will be able to control divine power for the benefit of others and ourselves.

But, as we shall see, the Holy Spirit as revealed in the Bible differs widely from the "Force." To help you understand the Spirit, I will provide a brief theological overview, beginning in the Old Testament, moving into the New Testament, and concluding with basic theological formulations from early Christian history.

The Holy Spirit in the Old Testament

The Holy Spirit appears at the beginning of creation, hovering above the primordial earth (Gen. 1:1–2). The Spirit, manifested as a wind from God, embodies the divine presence and power.

The Holy Spirit makes God's power available to people. Samson, the celebrated biblical strongman, does his feats of strength when the Spirit of the Lord comes upon him in power (Judg. 14:6, 19). King David's excellence in leadership comes from the Spirit (1 Sam. 16:13). When the Spirit rests upon the leaders of Israel, they prophesy (Num. 11:25; 1 Sam. 10:6). The Holy Spirit moved the Hebrew prophets to speak with divine authority (2 Peter 1:20–21).

One of the Old Testament prophets looked forward to a time when the Holy Spirit would inspire not only a few but a multitude of people:

"Then after I have poured out my rains again, I will pour out my Spirit upon all people. Your sons and daughters will prophesy. Your old men will dream dreams. Your young men will see visions. In those days, I will pour out my Spirit even on servants, men and women alike."

Joel 2:28–29

The Spirit of God will be poured out on people without respect to gender, age, or socioeconomic status. All will be inspired to see God's visions and to speak his words.

The Holy Spirit and Jesus

The New Testament associates Jesus with the Holy Spirit. His virgin mother becomes pregnant—a miraculous conception by the Spirit (Matt. 1:18–20; Luke 1:35). John the Baptist predicts that Jesus will baptize people with the Holy Spirit (Mark 1:8). Then, when John baptizes Jesus, the Spirit descends on Jesus like a dove (Mark 1:10). During his earthly ministry, Jesus is filled with and guided by the Spirit (Luke 4:1, 14). By the power of the Spirit, he casts out demons (Matt. 12:28).

Jesus sees the Holy Spirit not as his own unique endowment but as something to be given to others (Luke 11:13). After he dies and is resurrected, he will send the "Spirit of truth," who will bring glory to Jesus himself (John 16:14) and who will teach his followers everything they need to know (John 14:26; 15:26; 16:13).

After he is raised from the dead, Jesus instructs his followers to wait in Jerusalem until they are "baptized with the Holy Spirit" (Acts 1:4–5). Once this happens, they will be empowered to tell people everywhere about Jesus (Acts 1:8). Then, after Jesus ascended to heaven, his promise came true as the Holy Spirit was poured out on the first Christians at Pentecost. Joel's prophecy from centuries before was fulfilled (Acts 2:1–21). The Spirit came upon the believers in Jesus, giving birth to the church, empowering young and old, male and female, to minister through the power of God.

The Work of the Spirit Prior to Conversion

The New Testament is full of references to the Holy Spirit. Though no passage lays out a systematic theology of the Spirit, such a theology may be gleaned from many different passages taken together. The Holy Spirit begins to work in our lives before the moment of our conversion. In fact, the activity of the Spirit is required if we are to become Christians at all.

First, the Spirit is central to the whole process of communicating the good news about Jesus. The Holy Spirit empowers people so they will be able to bear witness to Jesus (Acts 1:8). Whenever the gospel is being shared, whether in a boisterous stadium jammed with people or in a quiet coffeehouse as two friends converse, the Holy Spirit is at work (1 Thess. 1:5).

Second, the Holy Spirit prepares us to receive the good news of salvation in Christ by making us aware of our need for him. Some of us knew right away when we heard the truth about Jesus that we needed to be saved from our sins. Others of us grew slowly into this realization. But, no matter what the exact process, it reflected the quiet work of God's Spirit (John 17:7–8).

Third, the Holy Spirit helps us commit our lives to Christ as our Lord. Even when we are sorry for our sin, we might still balk at recognizing Jesus as our Savior and Master. No matter how badly we have messed things up, we still like to run our own lives. Submitting to a Lord, even to one as gracious as Jesus, can be scary and can make us feel vulnerable. The Holy Spirit helps us do what we could not do by ourselves: "No one can say 'Jesus is Lord,' except by the Holy Spirit" (1 Cor. 12:3 NIV). Though someone could mouth the words "Jesus is Lord" without the Spirit's assistance, divine help is necessary if we are going to mean what we say.

Every Christian has experienced the power of the Holy Spirit. Many times we don't recognize the Spirit's guidance because it can be so gentle. No heavenly band plays "Hail to the Chief" when the Holy Spirit shows up. From our human vantage point, the Spirit's work leading to conversion can look like a series of coincidences. Sometimes people can identify the Spirit wooing them to embrace God's grace. Usually, however, we recognize the work of the Spirit only in retrospect.

The Work of the Spirit in Conversion

At the moment we come to faith in Jesus, the Spirit of God does several amazing things with us. First, the Spirit guarantees our future life with God (Eph. 1:13–14; 2 Cor. 5:5). God gives us the Holy Spirit to assure us that we truly belong to him. When we struggle with sin or doubt, the Spirit reminds us that God's claim on our lives will never be surrendered.

Second, in our conversion, the Holy Spirit gives us new birth and new life. Once we belong to Christ, he sends the Spirit, who "gives life to our mortal bodies" (Rom. 8:11). Jesus describes this process as being "born of water and the Spirit" (John 3:5 NIV). Paul echoes this insight in his letter to Titus: "[God] saved us, not because of the good things we did, but because of his mercy. He washed away our sins and gave us a new life through the Holy Spirit" (Titus 3:5). Though we continue to live with the same bodies in the same world, everything is suddenly different because we are different. It's as if we have begun life all over again. Therefore, "those who become Christians become new persons. They are not the same anymore, for the old life is gone. A new life has begun!" (2 Cor. 5:17).

The renewing work of the Spirit is rather like what happens to brand-new parents. The day my son Nathan was born, I was

37

forever changed. For the first time, I felt with the heart of a father. Here was this little person, someone I hardly knew, someone who would soon afflict me with sleeplessness and diapers. Yet I loved him more fiercely than I had ever loved anything or anyone. I was forever changed after only a few hours of parenthood. Since that time I have grown significantly in my parental identity. Psychologically speaking, I'm even more completely a father today than I was when Nathan was a newborn. But what happened on the momentous day of his birth made all the difference. My new way of living had begun.

So it is when the Holy Spirit gives us new birth. Throughout the rest of our lives, we will grow in our new identity as Christians. We don't make ourselves new through our own efforts. Rather, we work out the ramifications of a newness already given by the Holy Spirit.

Third, the Spirit joins us to the community of all other believers in Jesus. Paul explains this work of the Spirit to the Corinthians:

> Some of us are Jews, some are Gentiles, some are slaves, and some are free. But we have all been baptized into Christ's body by one Spirit, and we have all received the same Spirit.
>
> 1 Corinthians 12:13

When we come to faith in Christ, the Holy Spirit joins us to the community of believers in Jesus. From God's point of view, we are a part of the church not because we do anything but because of what the Holy Spirit has done at the moment of our conversion.

Fourth, the Holy Spirit comes to dwell within each believer and within the community of believers. The passage from 1 Corinthians that we just noted says, "we have all received the same Spirit" (1 Cor. 12:13). In another passage, Paul observes that "the Spirit of God, who raised Jesus from the dead, lives in you" (Rom. 8:11). Part of what distinguishes a Christian from the world is the presence of the Holy Spirit within the believer (John 14:16–17).

"But," you might ask, "what if I have no sensational experiences of the Holy Spirit, even though I believe in Jesus? Is it possible that I do not yet have the Holy Spirit?" Not according to Scripture: "Remember that those who do not have the Spirit of Christ living in them are not Christians at all" (Rom. 8:9). At times, the Spirit is revealed through signs and wonders, at other times through "a gentle whisper" (1 Kings 19:12 NIV). The nature of our experience does not prove the Spirit's presence within us. The clear word of Scripture does.

Because the Spirit of God is holy, those in whom the Spirit dwells are also holy, set apart for God and God's special purposes. Therefore, even our bodies take on a new sanctity (1 Cor. 6:19). If the Holy Spirit lives in you, your body is a temple for God, a place where God makes his presence known and where he is worshipped. Moreover, the gathered community of Christians also constitutes "the temple of God," the place where God's Spirit lives (1 Cor. 3:16–17).

The Holy Spirit as a Person of the Trinity

New Testament passages like the ones we have just referenced challenged early Christians to understand the nature of the Holy Spirit and the relationship between the Spirit and God. Many New Testament texts underline the intimate connection between God and the Spirit, adding Jesus into the equation as well. Jesus himself says, "Therefore, go and make disciples of all the nations, baptizing them in the name of the Father and the Son and the Holy Spirit" (Matt. 28:19; see also Matt. 3:16–17; John 14:16; 15:26; Gal. 4:6; 1 Peter 1:2). As Christians in the first centuries after Christ wrestled with biblical affirmations about the Spirit, they searched for a way to talk about God that affirmed the divinity of the Father, the Son, and the Holy Spirit. Yet they also held on tenaciously to the core Jewish belief that there is only one God. How could God be one but also, in some sense, three?

By the close of the fourth century A.D., the church established what has become the norm for Christian belief ever since: the doctrine of the Trinity. Simply stated, we believe in one God who exists in three persons, Father, Son, and Holy Spirit. These three persons are essential to God, just as three musicians are essential to a trio. Take one away, and you don't have a trio anymore. Take away one person from God, and you don't have God. But, unlike the three musicians, the persons of God share completely in the same being, the same essence. They are not separate beings the way three singers are distinct. The Father, Son, and Holy Spirit are profoundly and permanently one.

Among its nuances, the personal language for the Trinity indicates that we can have a relationship with each person of the Godhead, with Father, Son, and Holy Spirit. The Holy Spirit is not some impersonal power. Christians often refer to the Holy Spirit with the male pronoun "he." This emphasizes personality, not gender, because the Holy Spirit is neither male nor female. The Spirit is not an "it" or a "thing" or a "higher power." Rather, the Spirit is a person with whom we can have a relationship, a relationship Paul describes with the word *koinōnia,* even as John spoke of our having *koinōnia* with the Father and the Son (1 John 1:3).

What is "The *Koinōnia* of the Spirit"?

When Paul prays that the Corinthians experience "the *koinōnia* of the Spirit," he exploits an inherent ambiguity in Greek grammar. The fellowship of the Spirit can be the fellowship we have *with* the Spirit, or it can be fellowship with other Christians *provided by* the Spirit. I believe Paul has both meanings in mind.

Elsewhere in his writings, Paul reveals that the Holy Spirit lives in us (Rom. 8:11). The indwelling Spirit reassures us that we are God's children (Rom. 8:16), helps us when we are weak (Rom. 8:26), prays for us when we don't have the words (Rom. 8:26), leads us (Rom. 8:14), teaches us (1 Cor. 2:21), and gives us inner strength and joy (Eph. 3:16; 1 Thess. 1:6). Through the Spirit, God's love is poured into our hearts (Rom. 5:5). When he prays for the Corinthians, Paul desires that they experience all of these dimensions of fellowship with the Spirit, and many more besides.

But this doesn't exhaust Paul's meaning. The Holy Spirit also draws us into the fellowship among Christians that he creates and nurtures. At Pentecost, the Spirit gives birth to the church (Acts 2), which becomes a temple in which he dwells. In our conversion, the Spirit immerses us into the community of Christ (1 Cor. 12:12–13). Through empowering individual believers, the Spirit builds up the body of Christ (1 Corinthians 14). Paul wishes that the Corinthians would experience the full *koinōnia* of the Spirit by sharing life together in the power of the Spirit.

Not surprisingly, Paul's sense of *koinōnia* agrees with that of John in his first letter. As we saw in Chapter 1, the Christian life is intimate fellowship with God (Father and Son) and with God's people. Paul would add that that Christian life is also intimate fellowship with the Spirit of God and with the community of the Spirit. Both New Testament writers use the language of *koinōnia* to underscore the inseparability of a relationship with God and a relationship with the people of God.

41

Koinōnia with the Spirit Leads to *Koinōnia* with Christians

Sometimes we mistakenly associate true spirituality with unending solitude. We imagine that a deep relationship with the Holy Spirit turns people into religious ascetics who live alone on some inaccessible mountaintop to revel in mystical solitude. Nothing could be further from the truth. Though solitude is one essential component of Christian experience, it is not the ultimate goal of the spiritual life. In fact, the more deeply we grow in the Spirit, the more deeply we will know one another.

I learned this lesson through a life-transforming experience many years ago. I had always been in awe of Henri Nouwen's spiritual depth. His many writings inspired myriads of Christians, including me, to pursue a deeper relationship with God. You can probably imagine, therefore, how excited I was when my friend Tod arranged to have lunch with Nouwen and invited me to join them.

I had a hidden agenda for our conversation, however. I was in the throes of writing my dissertation, and it was not going well. Living three thousand miles away from Harvard, I was trying to negotiate a tricky long-distance relationship with my professors. When my third advisor in three years told me that my work was "a bunch of bunk" and that I must read a 350-page tome written only in dense German prose, I felt certain my project was doomed. Meanwhile, I was loving my work in the church and was aware that I would never need a doctorate to fulfill my primary pastoral calling.

I had just about decided to quit my degree program when Tod invited me to lunch with him and my spiritual hero. It occurred to me that Nouwen might be able to confirm my decision to terminate my doctoral work because he had recently left Harvard to become a pastor for mentally disabled adults.

When our lunch date with Nouwen finally arrived, I planned to bring up the issue without showing my hand, not to mention my heart. I began with what seemed like a safe question.

"Henri," I said, "how has it been for you to leave Harvard behind? Do you feel fulfilled in your pastoral work here? Or do you miss academic life?"

Henri didn't answer right away. His mind seemed to be churning. Then he turned to me, looked me square in the eyes as if he could peer into my soul, and asked bluntly, "What is it you *really* want to ask? What do you *really* want to know?"

His question struck like a bolt of lightning. He *could* see into my soul. In a moment, he moved from the periphery of my guarded heart right into the core. Casual conversation all of a sudden became intimate fellowship.

"Well," I stammered, "I guess I do have a real question. Here's my situation. . . ." I proceeded to outline my dissertation woes and my decision to leave it all behind. I looked to him for some kind of affirming word.

Without hesitation, Henri responded, "Whatever you do, you absolutely must finish your dissertation and complete your degree. For you this is essential. Once you're done, you never have to return to academia again. But, first you have to finish."

I felt as if I had heard the voice of God. Henri didn't say, "Thus says the Lord," because he didn't have to. The Lord was speaking. And, frankly, I was not happy with what I heard. I felt disappointed and afraid.

I can't remember much about the rest of that meal or the conversation. I was overcome by the realization that my life had been fundamentally changed by the direct word of a relative stranger as we shared a pepperoni pizza. In retrospect, I realize how right Henri was. Had I quit my doctoral program, something in me would have remained unfinished and restless. Many of the professional doors that have been opened by my degree would have been shut to me.

At the time of our conversation, I wondered how Henri could have spoken so insightfully; after all, he hardly knew me. The answer now seems obvious. Henri's intimacy with God opened a window of intimacy with me. His sensitivity to the Holy Spirit allowed him to be sensitive to me in a miraculous way. The depth of Henri's relationship with God had not distanced him from others but had led to far deeper relationships with them.

The example of Henri Nouwen illustrates one other implication of our fellowship with the Holy Spirit. "Spirituality" is in these days. Most secular bookstores have several of Nouwen's books on the shelves. Just about everybody wants to be "spiritual," whatever that means. Most popular spiritualities make no pretense of being Christian. It is trendy for Christians to be "into" spirituality. This sounds positive, but many Christians have allowed the culture to define their notions of "spirituality." One result is that believers can be "into" spirituality rather than "into" God.

Christian spirituality can be viewed from many different perspectives. There is certainly no "one right way" to envision such an intricate and vast subject. But, at its core, *Christian spirituality is life in the Spirit.* It is intimate fellowship with the Holy Spirit, shared with others to whom we are joined by that same Spirit.

PRACTICAL QUESTIONS AND ANSWERS
1. "How can I learn more about the Holy Spirit?"

Of course, the best source of reliable information about the Holy Spirit is the Bible. I recommend that you study the following biblical passages in depth: Luke 1; Acts 2; Romans 8; 1 Cor-inthians 12–14; Galatians 5–6; 1 John 4.

The following books on the Spirit are insightful and trustwor-thy: Gordon D. Fee, Paul, the Spirit, and the People of God *(Peabody: Hendrickson Publishers, 1996); Michael Green,* I Believe in the Holy Spirit *(Grand Rapids: Eerdmans, 1975, reprint 1992).*

2. "How can I develop a spirituality that is distinctively Christian?"

True Christian spirituality focuses on God, not on yourself, or on freeing your mind, or on certain particular spiritual exer-cises. To know God more deeply, we need to study and medi-tate on his self-revelation in Scripture. Alongside of Bible read-ing, prayer is a primary discipline of Christian spirituality. For an excellent introduction to Christian spirituality, see Richard Foster's Celebration of Discipline: The Path to Spiritual Growth, *3d ed. (San Francisco: HarperSanFrancisco, 1998).*

45

3
Intimate Fellowship
in the Body of Christ

On the day of Pentecost, the Holy Spirit was poured out on the small band of Jesus' followers. One of them, a fisherman named Peter, stood up to preach the first Christian sermon. When he finished, three thousand people put their faith in Jesus as the one who would save them from their sins (Acts 2:41). Three thousand converts—not a bad start for a brand-new preacher who didn't even graduate from seminary.

What did these converts do? Immediately, they were baptized and joined the community of Christians. They "devoted themselves to the teaching of the apostles, to intimate fellowship, to the breaking of bread, and to prayer" (Acts 2:42 MDR). Here, right at the very beginning of Christian history, we find *koinōnia*. The earliest believers in Jesus seemed to know by intuition that the Christian life was something to be shared with other believers. They didn't simply add some new religious beliefs to their worldview and go on with life as usual. Nor did they immediately withdraw from the crowd to engage in private devotions. Rather, they embraced the community of other Christians as that community embraced them.

The behavior of the first believers in Jesus stands in contrast to the pattern so common among Christians in North America. Certainly a few of us express our newfound faith in Christ by joining some Christian group. Many of us, however, stand back from churches and other Christian organizations, sometimes confused about how to connect, sometimes doubtful that such connection is necessary, sometimes even fearful that sharing with other Christians will dilute the intense reality of our faith.

Some of us started out in relationship with other Christians but later backed away from the Christian community. Perhaps life was simply too busy to keep church participation on the list of pressing priorities. Perhaps we were disappointed by Christians who failed to live according to the example of Jesus. I remember one woman complaining bitterly about the inadequacies of a Christian group: "We have such a hard time getting along. It's crazy! The church is supposed to be like a family!" My response took her by surprise. "That's exactly the problem," I said. "We *are* a family. How many families do you know that live in perfect harmony?" However valid my point, it doesn't exactly make one want to run out and join a church!

Almost every survey of American spirituality concludes that, while the vast majority of Americans believe in God, only a minority regularly attend religious services. Among those who attend, a much smaller percentage actually become meaningfully involved in the life of a religious community. For us, personal faith means private faith. If I choose to share it with someone else, that's my choice. It's certainly not expected or required. Many Americans are downright suspicious of the influence of religious communities. In a recent survey, 80 percent of Americans (including many self-confessed Christians) agreed that "an individual should arrive at his or her own religious beliefs independent of any churches or synagogues."[1] If we choose our beliefs all by ourselves, then we have every right to practice these beliefs all by ourselves.

The privatization of faith reflects the individualism that dwells deep in the American soul. Though we like to join lots of voluntary organizations and have lots of casual friendships, we are wary of committing ourselves in a way that might compromise our freedom. For many Christians, this becomes a license to avoid church and other forms of Christian community. How different we tend to be from the first Christians who followed up their Pentecost conversion by joining in *koinōnia* with other believers.

Corinthian Individualism and Paul's Response

We are very much like some other Christians we read about in the New Testament. The apostle Paul planted a church in the Greek city of Corinth. After spending a year and a half there, his ministry took him elsewhere. But Paul continued to receive reports about the Corinthian church, reports that distressed him. Those new Christians were doing what comes naturally, adapting their Christian life to the values of their culture. In the process, they were losing touch with the intimate fellowship that ought to characterize Christian living.

Because Paul could not travel to Corinth right away to set things right, he wrote a letter we know as 1 Corinthians. In his introduction to the letter, he reminds the recipients of their privileged relationship with Christ and his people: "God is faithful, through whom you were called into the intimate fellowship *[koinōnia]* of his Son Jesus Christ our Lord" (1 Cor. 1:9 MDR).

This fellowship was threatened by the individualistic attitudes of the Corinthians. "As long as I get my religious jolt every now and then, that's all that really matters," they were saying. One man believed his Christian freedom gave him the right to live in a sexual relationship with his stepmother (1 Cor. 5:1). Others thought it was just fine for them to eat meat served in pagan temples, even if their behavior was hurting other members of the church (1 Corinthians 8). Some of the Corinthians took pride in their spiritual prowess, putting down others who were lacking powerful demonstrations (1 Corinthians 12–14).

Before we condemn the Corinthians for their self-centeredness, however, we should notice how much we resemble them. Not only do we let our culture warp our Christianity but we also tend to echo the "It's all fine as long as I get mine" individualism of Corinth.

Paul could have tried to correct the Corinthian problem by giving a quick series of commands: "Don't sleep with your stepmother. Don't eat in pagan temples. Don't boast about your spiritual endowments." But he wanted to do more than rebuke the Corinthians and redirect their behavior.

In his letter, Paul seeks to instruct the church so that its behavior might flow from solid Christian theology. Rather than simply shouting, "Don't be individualistic," Paul helps the Corinthians comprehend who they are as a community formed by God. He does this by using the image of the human body:

> The human body has many parts, but the many parts make up only one body. So it is with the body of Christ. Some of us are Jews, some are Gentiles, some are slaves, and some are free. But we have all been baptized into Christ's body by one Spirit, and we have all received the same Spirit.
>
> 1 Corinthians 12:12–13

Paul's baptismal metaphor guarantees that we don't consider our connection to the body as something extrinsic and temporary.

Our connection to the body depends on God's action through the Spirit, not on our own activity. Whether we choose to live in light of what God has done is another story. But, if you are a vital organ that has been transplanted into Christ's body, you can see how risky it would be for you to live apart from that body. Both the body of Christ and your own life will be strengthened through your connection, but weakened if you amputate yourself from the body.

We Are Diverse Yet United

The human body has many different parts, yet it is one unified body. This basic anatomical fact reveals the folly of wanting all members of Christ's body to be the same. "Suppose the whole body were an eye," Paul suggests, "then how would you hear? Or if your whole body were just one big ear, how could you smell anything? What a strange thing a body would be if it had only one part" (1 Cor. 12:17, 19). What a hilarious image! Just picture the human body as a giant collection of ears, or as one big eye—hardly a body at all! Those Corinthians who devalued the contribution of others because it was not like their own stood corrected by the humorous picture of a monstrous eye.

Yet, if the parts of the body differ, that does not make them separate from one another, because "the many parts make up only one body" (1 Cor. 12:12). Each individual part of the body is necessarily connected to the whole body. In the body of Christ, the distinct parts, so variable and different from one another, are unified as one body (1 Cor. 12:27). It's that simple: one body, many parts; one unified body made up of diverse parts.

That's easy to say, I might add, but not to do. Most Christian communities have a very difficult time living with diversity. Uniformity is so much more comfortable. If we all look about the same, dress the same, talk in the same way, and vote the same, we find it so much easier to get along. If we all agree on music style and sermon length, worship wars are fought on somebody else's turf, not our own. But, unfortunately for our comfort, that's not what it means to be the church of Jesus Christ. God has intentionally created the body of Christ to be diverse. In our efforts to remake it according to our own need for uniformity, we end up like Victor Frankenstein, creating a monster rather than the body designed by God.

We Are a Body Standing on Its Head

Paul was not the first writer of his day to use the metaphor of the body in reference to human community. Defenders of the Roman Empire argued that it was like a human body. From this insight they bolstered the oppressive Roman hierarchy. The head must remain on top, they argued, served by the bowels of the Empire.[2]

In contrast to his Roman contemporaries, Paul portrays the body of Christ as if it were doing a headstand. The lower parts receive the honor usually given to the higher parts (1 Cor. 12:22–24). That's the way God designed it. By turning the body upside down, Paul rebukes those Corinthians who boasted of their spiritual accomplishments. The ones they would consider less honorable are, in fact, worthy of greater honor. The unworthy stomach gets the limelight, while the apparently glorious head gets the shadows.

If you spend time in a healthy church, you'll see this inversion repeatedly. When I was an associate pastor at Hollywood Presbyterian Church, I was responsible for the educational ministries. Now and then I'd wander around on Sunday mornings, checking on classes for all ages. Once I peeked into a classroom for three-year-olds. Sitting on the floor was an immaculately dressed woman who was reading a story to a group of children. In her professional life, this woman was a vice president of one of the country's most prestigious corporations. But, as she got down on a three-year-old's level, only her clothing gave away her worldly success. Within the body of Christ, this powerful, honorable woman was a humble servant of powerless, undistinguished children.

We Depend on One Another

In the church of Jesus Christ, the less honorable parts of the body of Christ are worthy of greater honor, and "all members care for each other equally" (1 Cor. 12:25). This vision of mutual care sounds idyllic. Yet as we begin to think about the implications, we might start wondering, "All the members have the same care for one another? How is this possible? Paul, are you sure?"

To grasp Paul's point here, we must know something about the church in the first century. The word *church* conjures up a clear picture in our minds: a distinctive building with religious symbolism, members sitting in rows facing an altar or stage, and identified leaders who do most of the ministry for the members who receive it. None of these features would have been found in first-century churches. Christians gathered primarily in homes, with the maximum size determined by the house (usually, fifty people or less). Members sat or stood to face one another, not in rows facing a stage. Leadership was shared by all the church members, with each expected to minister as led by the Spirit.

Consequently, when Paul calls all the members to care for one another equally, he does not envision an American megachurch with thousands of members and dozens of professional staff, or even the typical congregation with a couple hundred members and one pastor. Paul pictures something much more like contemporary small groups, intimate circles of people who worship, pray, and learn together.

Though our contemporary forms of church differ considerably from Paul's, we shouldn't dismiss his call for mutual care, even if this contradicts our expectations for church. Many people go to church to receive professional care from professional clergy. They want excellent teaching, inspirational leadership, and tender pastoral care. These expectations are legitimate. But, in biblical perspective, those who receive such benefits should also give them to others. My job as pastor is to provide pastoral care that equips each member of my church to care for others (Eph. 4:12).

We Share the Full Range of Human Emotions Together

Earlier in this book we noted that *koinōnia* leads to complete joy. But joy is not the only emotion we share together in the body of Christ. Paul notes: "If one part suffers, all the parts suffer with it, and if one part is honored, all the parts are glad" (1 Cor. 12:26). We share in gladness, to be sure, but also in suffering and sorrow.

There is a double challenge embedded in Paul's call to broad-ranging empathy. First of all, we should note our calling to suffer along with those who suffer. The text doesn't say anything about making them feel better. We are told simply to hurt with those who hurt. This can be much harder than merely giving comfort. Sometimes I'd rather just cheer people up and be on my merry way.

Americans are becoming understandably cynical about compassion these days. Conservatives mock one president of the United States for trying to "feel our pain." Liberals deride the next president for advocating "compassionate conservatism." Of course, we should be wary of people who fake compassion to promote their own agendas, no matter what their political persuasion. But we mustn't let wariness harden our hearts, turning us away from God's call to genuine compassion, to hurting with those who hurt. As members of Christ's body, we must share one another's sorrows.

For me, the second challenge inherent in Paul's picture of the sympathetic body is even more unsettling. If, when one part suffers, all the parts suffer with it, then when I suffer, others should suffer along with me. This implies that I must let them know when I am suffering. If there's one thing I like less than feeling pain, it's admitting that pain to other people. I want to pretend that I am above it all, a man of strength and unwavering faith. I don't want to be weak, needy, or vulnerable. Yet God expects me to share my suffering with members of Christ's body. He expects it, I fear, because he knows we cannot bear our pain alone. We have been created to share such things with others.

Perhaps you are not cursed with the need to pretend that you're invincible. But, as a pastor, I know that my reticence to share my pain is not unique. Often, when members of my church go into the hospital, they won't tell anyone because they are embarrassed. Or they will struggle silently as their family crumbles but keep it to themselves because they feel so ashamed. When folks in my church hide their pain, I feel frustrated because they make it impossible for the body to care for them as it should. But I certainly relate to the fears that keep folks from admitting their struggles.

There have been times in my life, however, when my suffering has been so acute that I couldn't hide it. Fifteen years ago my dad was dying of cancer, slowly and excruciatingly. In the last stages of his life, my family and I would nurse my dad, caring for him in ways that sapped every ounce of our strength. The combination of sadness and stress was almost too much to bear. Thank God, we didn't have to bear it alone!

I was working at Hollywood Presbyterian Church during those years, the church where my parents had been active for two decades. During the last year of my father's life, friends from church would check in with me and my family each day. They prayed without ceasing. They loved without expecting anything in return. In my dad's last three months, they began bringing dinners to my parents' home, every night a new meal. The food ranged from perfectly cooked prime rib to take-out fried chicken. Every meal communicated love that fed our souls as well as our bodies. Experiences like this one have made it a bit easier for me to share my sufferings with others, but only a bit!

Let me add that such intimacy will not happen, and is not meant to happen, in large groups. It's impossible for groups larger than forty or fifty to suffer and rejoice together in the manner Paul envisions. If we are to be active members of the body of Christ, therefore, we must be in groups that are small enough to facilitate mutual sharing. Most churches have groups like this. They go by different names, such as small groups, cell groups, growth groups, adult classes, home Bible studies, kinship groups, prayer groups. Specific group functions differ from church to church. Most of these gatherings facilitate personal openness, providing a place for people to share their pains and their victories.

There is a more appealing upside to Paul's vision of body sympathy: if one part is honored, all the parts are glad. The Corinthians were mired in self-centered accomplishment, seeking to magnify their own honor, even at the expense of others. God's plan for the body of Christ eliminates all of this

55

selfish striving. If we share all of life together, the honoring of a fellow body part will feel like we're honoring ourselves.

Fellowship with Other Christians Contributes to Fellowship with God and Vice Versa

We have seen how fellowship with other Christians supports us in difficult times, keeping us in touch with God when he seems far away. But this is just the beginning. Participation in the body of Christ enriches every aspect of our relationship with God.

A couple of examples will help illustrate this point. Members of my church often make mission trips to northern Mexico, visiting orphans, building simple homes, feeding the hungry, and sharing the good news of Jesus. They are able to participate in these ministries because they are part of a Christian community. It's unlikely that they would be able to do such things by themselves, even if they wanted to. Of course, those who receive the direct benefits of their service are greatly blessed. But so are those who serve. To a person, they speak of how their own relationship with God has come alive through caring for others. This growth in personal faith is facilitated through fellowship with other Christians.

The second example of how *koinōnia* with people inspires *koinōnia* with God comes from corporate worship. All Christians join together to remember the death of Jesus through the symbolic use of bread and wine (or grape juice, as in most Protestant traditions). We call what we do by different names: "The Lord's Supper," "The Eucharist," "The Sacrament," "The Mass," or "communion." This last title, "communion," comes from the Latin translation of the Greek word *koinōnia*. When we share in the bread and the cup, we have intimate fellowship.

Not surprisingly, the Corinthian Christians tended to focus on their own individualistic experience as they shared in the symbolic bread and wine. Paul rebuked their self-centeredness and called them to care for one another in the midst of their sacramental supper (1 Cor. 11:17–34). His theological basis for this exhortation uses the Greek word *koinōnia:*

> The cup of blessing that we bless [in the Lord's Supper], is it not intimate fellowship *[koinōnia]* with the blood of Christ? The bread that we break, is it not intimate fellowship *[koinōnia]* with the body of Christ? Because there is one bread, we, though we are many, are one body, for we all share in the one bread.
>
> 1 Corinthians 10:16–17 MDR

The word *koinōnia* in this passage, often translated as "communion," refers to the deep relationship we have with Jesus when we receive his supper. When we receive communion, we have intimate fellowship with Christ's blood and body. We remember his death for us and share once again in its benefits by the power of the Holy Spirit.

But that's not the total of our fellowship in the Lord's Supper. Our *koinōnia* with the body of Christ is not only remembrance of Jesus' death but also fellowship with the present body of Christ, with the church gathered together for the Lord's Supper. In sharing the bread together, "we, though we are many, are one." When we receive the Lord's Supper, therefore, we have communion both with Jesus and with one another. We share in the fullness of intimate fellowship.

In this case, *koinōnia* with other believers fosters deeper *koinōnia* with God, and vice versa. When we receive communion in church, our personal relationship with God is strengthened. Moreover, our communion with Christ through the bread and the cup strengthens our communion with one another. We are delivered from an individualism that limits our fellowship with God. We are stretched so that we might know the fullness of intimate fellowship, both with God and with God's people.

Practical Questions and Answers

1. "My church is a good one, but I'm having a hard time getting connected. What can I do?"

Have you made a serious attempt to be connected, or are you circling around the outside without jumping in? If you stay on the fringes of any church, you will feel like an outsider. Chances are good that you will end up leaving that church. If you want to be connected, you need to commit yourself to some context for genuine relationships.

I recently spoke with a woman who was leaving my church because she "just didn't connect with the people." I asked her where she had tried to fit in: Women's Ministry? "No." Sunday morning adult class? "No." Midweek Bible study? "No, not enough time." Small group Bible study? "No." In truth, she simply hadn't made an effort to get involved with people. She was "too busy," which is another way of saying she didn't value relationships with other Christians highly enough to make it happen. Be honest with yourself and choose to make real participation in church a high priority in your life.

2. "I'm a member of a church, but it's pretty dead. What should I do?"

There's no quick or simple answer to this question. I believe that God wants to bring new life to dying churches. Renewal comes through the Holy Spirit, usually as church members share their excitement about the Lord with others. But this process of church renewal can be slow and frustrating.

If you're in a church that seems to be dead, the first thing to do is to pray for God's help and guidance. Pray for your church, its leadership, its members. Pray for the Spirit to blow freely and freshly through the congregation. Ask the Lord if there are ways he wants to use you to bring new life to your church.

Second, look for others in the church who are passionate about the Lord. Even struggling churches usually have a small cadre of saints who have walked with Christ for years and are faithful to the church. Often these folks are senior citizens with mature faith and tender hearts. If possible, meet regularly with these people to pray for each other and for the church.

Third, try to understand why your church is dying. Sometimes churches have a terminal theological disease. Is the gospel of Christ preached in the sermons? Does the Bible provide authoritative direction for church leadership? Do those who plan and lead worship attempt to honor God, even if their attempts aren't very successful? If your church appears to have severe theological problems, I'd encourage you to speak with the pastor. Find out what's really going on. If church leaders have given up on orthodox Christian faith, renewal of that church will be extraordinarily difficult.

Fourth, if you believe that God is calling you to find another church, leave your former church with gratitude and grace. Don't get caught up in a spirit of judgmentalism and criticism.

4

Intimate Fellowship and the Bible

Nothing strikes terror in the hearts of parents like three simple words: "Some assembly required." We shop carefully to find just the right toy for our daughter's birthday. Yet somehow we overlook those fateful words, printed on toy boxes like high voltage warnings on power poles: "Some assembly required." Translated realistically, this means, "Warning! Parents keep away! Danger!" Nevertheless, we pay our money and then pay the real price when our daughter opens a box that contains, not a cute little dollhouse, but a pile of parts that promises to drive us crazy.

Yet for those of us who attempt the impossible, there is hope: the directions that promise to show us how to turn that mysterious mess of pieces into a quaint dollhouse. We want to trust the instructions, believing that the same folks who created those pieces were also the authors of the booklet. If anyone can help us get the toy into working order, it will be the ones who made the toy.

Our initial faith in the direction book is soon challenged by its contents. Even when we finally locate the instructions in English, we still confront sentences so complex that they require decoding: "Insert screw J through hole Y, with washer S and lock washer P, into nut W." Advanced degrees in linguistics and engineering are required just to figure out the instructions.

If you'll pardon my simplistic analogy, life is rather like a child's toy. The picture on the box looks intriguing, but life doesn't come fully assembled. Our job as human beings is to put together a life worth living.

This is no easy task. It requires much more than "*some* assembly." But there is hope for us as we start piecing together our lives. Life comes with directions. Our Creator has not abandoned us to our own devices but has given us instructions for assembling an abundant life.

Many of us would rather do it ourselves. We think we can figure out how to put together a meaningful life without outside help. But, we inevitably confront challenges that exceed our intuition. When we stand back and look at the life we've created, we recognize that our masterpiece is a mess. Some of us proudly display the trappings of success, but inside we feel like failures. We send perfectly posed pictures in our Christmas cards while our families disintegrate. We teach our children not to cheat in school while we cheat on our income tax. Our lives aren't anything like the picture on the box.

In the midst of failing to construct the lives we want to live, we realize that some directions for building would be helpful. At this point, many of us look to the Bible for assistance. We sense that, without divine directions, we'll never put life together right. It's time to get some authoritative help.

Why Trust the Bible?

Many of us would answer this question by pointing to the lives of Christians we know. People who live according to biblical teachings tend to do better than those who don't. They are like hikers with a map and compass, people who don't get lost nearly as often as those who blaze a trail without any idea of where they are going.

Personal testimonies to biblical trustworthiness are compelling, but I want to look at the Bible's own claims rather than merely recount individual stories. The stories are persuasive, but they rest on the bedrock of theological truth, a summary of which we find in Paul's second letter to his protégé, Timothy. Timothy was serving as a pastor during a difficult time, when the church was struggling with persecution from the outside and false teaching on the inside. Paul urges Timothy to "remain faithful" to the things he was taught in Scripture:

> You have been taught the holy Scriptures from childhood, and they have given you the wisdom to receive the salvation that comes by trusting in Christ Jesus. All Scripture is inspired by God and is useful to teach us what is true and to make us realize what is wrong in our lives. It straightens us out and teaches us to do what is right. It is God's way of preparing us in every way, fully equipped for every good thing God wants us to do.
>
> 2 Timothy 3:15–17

The Bible can be trusted, Paul explains, because it is "inspired by God." The Spirit of God has breathed divine truth into the Scripture. Of course, God's Word comes in the form of human words. Thus, Scripture is both human and divine. This is a mystery we'll never understand fully, rather like incarnation of the Word of God in Jesus. The Bible is a human book, written by human beings in their languages, styles, and influenced by their cultures. Yet it is also a divine book, one in which God has breathed and through which God continues to speak. The Bible is, therefore, eminently trustworthy and ultimately authoritative for our faith and actions, even though it is a historical document written by people who lived centuries ago.

Just as the directions for assembling a toy are trustworthy because they were written by the maker of the toy, so it is with the Bible. The same God who created us is the God who shows us how to live. Therefore, we echo the words of the psalmist:

> How sweet are your words to my taste;
> they are sweeter than honey.
> Your commandments give me understanding;
> no wonder I hate every false way of life.
> Your word is a lamp for my feet
> and a light for my path.
>
> Psalm 119:103–105

"But," we might wonder, "what about other authorities? What about science, medicine, philosophy, psychology, and just plain common sense? If we accept the Bible as uniquely true, must we reject other possible guides to life?" It all depends on how we follow these other guides. As Christians, we believe that the Bible contains Truth with a capital "T." But we don't claim that all truths are found in Scripture. We can use our God-given abilities to discover countless truths that the Bible does not mention. For example, you can certainly use the directions for assembling a toy without compromising the ultimate authority of Scripture for your life.

The crucial issue has to do not with adjunct authorities for living but with ultimate authority. If we believe that the Bible has been given to us as a uniquely authoritative source of truth, then we should recognize the supreme authority of

Scripture over other guides when they deal with issues found within the Bible, and especially when they disagree with biblical teaching.

Take the controversial case of human sexuality, for example. The Bible teaches that sex is a good gift of God to be enjoyed only in the context of marriage between a man and a woman. Sex outside of marriage is revealed to be wrong. Many contemporary authorities, however, claim that sexual intimacy should not be limited to the marriage relationship. We face disagreement among rival authorities and must decide which authority deserves our ultimate allegiance.

Many people who are not Christians, and even a few Christians, give preference to the "conclusions of modern science and psychology." "The Bible is old-fashioned," they argue, "trapped within ancient culture. We should be guided by new insights." This argument makes two unwarranted assumptions. First, it assumes a unity and an objectivity among modern theories that are nowhere to be found if one actually studies these theories. Second, and more significantly, it assumes that the Bible's antiquity weakens its contemporary authority; modern ideology, no matter how fleeting, confused, and contradictory it might be, is enthroned as the trustworthy guide for life simply because it is recent. Yet there is no valid argument that proves something is irrelevant simply because it's old.

In our postmodern world, many have lost faith in "modern science and psychology." They see these disciplines not as purveyors of objective truth but as human constructs that are fraught with subjectivity. Just like the rest of us, scientists and psychologists project their own values into their investigations. What is left to guide us if objectivity cannot be found? Feelings! The ultimate guide for living becomes our personal, subjective, gut instinct. If I *feel* that sex outside of marriage is okay, then it is, for me. If you *feel* differently, then that is your right. Moral authority resides in our emotional states and cannot be generalized for all people.

Both modernism and postmodernism simply assume that God has not spoken authoritatively in the Bible. They dismiss scriptural authority, not so much by reasoned arguments, as by faith in modern science or postmodern feelings. If, however, God has actually breathed truth into the Bible, such a dismissal is unwarranted and downright foolish. If God has done what the Bible claims, Scripture deserves to reign over our thoughts, emotions, and actions, even if it contradicts modernist faith or postmodern sentiment.

Of course, we cannot prove the ultimate authority of the Bible in a way that would convince a die-hard skeptic. A person who wants a reason to reject scriptural authority can always find one. That's not to say our commitment to biblical authority cannot be defended. Faithful scholarship underscores the trustworthiness of the Bible, pointing to the overwhelming number of manuscripts that guarantee its authenticity, or to the archaeological evidence that supports its reliability. The obvious pragmatic benefits of scriptural guidance strengthen the case for accepting the Bible's authority. But, after all of the evidence has been sifted, each person faces a choice that demands a step beyond what can be proved. Those who have chosen to put their weight down on the supreme authority of Scripture have found it to be solid, an incomparable foundation for life's journey.

The Purposes of the Whole Bible

According to Paul's advice to Timothy that we examined above, Scripture has two basic purposes. First, it leads us to salvation. Second, it prepares us for living well.

When we think of the Bible bringing us to salvation, we naturally focus on the New Testament. But the whole Bible, not only the New Testament, points to Jesus Christ and leads us to salvation through him. The "holy Scriptures" that guided Timothy to salvation were what we call the Old Testament, because the New Testament documents weren't written when he was a child. Even though the two testaments differ in certain respects, there is a fundamental unity between them. Both reveal God's salvation and help us receive that salvation through Jesus (1 Cor. 15:1–4).

The Bible prepares us to live well (2 Tim. 3:16–17). It teaches us the truth and how to do what is right. It equips us "for every good thing God wants us to do." When we err, it shows us what is wrong and "straightens us out."

Though we might appreciate positive instruction, we don't enjoy being rebuked and corrected. Given what Paul says about the Bible, therefore, we should expect it to make us unhappy at times; unhappy, but also much wiser. According to the Book of Proverbs, "If you listen to constructive criticism, you will be at home among the wise. If you reject criticism, you only harm yourself" (15:31–32a). In fact, sometimes the rebuke of Scripture leads not only to wisdom but even to joy.

Several years ago, I was preaching on an Old Testament passage in which the Lord says, "I hate divorce" (Mal. 2:16). I connected this passage to the teaching of Jesus, calling my congregation to a new commitment to marriage. As I greeted folks after the service, I heard the usual collection of "Nice sermon, pastor" comments.

The next morning I received an altogether different kind of response. A man named Jeff called me at church. He had been at the worship service the day before and had a desperate need to speak with me. He didn't want to elaborate but said it had to do with my sermon. I rearranged my schedule so I could visit with him during his lunch hour.

"Your sermon really upset me," Jeff began.

Oh no, not a great start to this conversation, I thought quietly, as I steeled myself for criticism.

"What you said about marriage and divorce has completely messed me up," he continued. He then told me his story. A couple years ago, he had begun an affair with a coworker. When his wife discovered his unfaithfulness, Jeff left his wife and two small children and moved in with his girlfriend. Shortly thereafter, he began divorce proceedings. At the time of our lunch meeting, everything was final, except one last signature. With the sweep of a pen, Jeff's marriage would be completely over.

Until the day before, Jeff had never really questioned the morality of his actions. He was sorry to hurt his wife's feelings and especially those of his children. But he was tired of his marriage and in love with his coworker. Then, owing to a number of "coincidences," Jeff had visited our church the day before, only to hear my sermon on marriage and divorce.

"For the first time I wonder what God thinks about what I've done," Jeff continued. "Maybe I shouldn't get divorced. Maybe I should try to get back with my wife, though by now she hates my guts. I don't know what to do. What do you think I should do?"

I tried in a gracious way to explain to this man what God intended for marriage and God's consequent hatred of divorce (even though it is something God has allowed in some circumstances and which God forgives even when it is completely wrong). I agreed that Jeff's wife might very well have no interest in reconciliation but encouraged him to talk with her. She was a Christian, I discovered, as was Jeff, though he had not been living in fellowship with God for many years. As Jeff and I prayed together, I pleaded with God for help. Neither of us felt a lightning bolt from heaven that promised healing for his marriage, but we sensed God's support for an effort to reconcile.

Ten months later, I found myself praying with Jeff once again. The previous months had been an emotional roller coaster for him and his wife. At first she laughed off his offer to reconcile. But, after a while, she sensed a change in Jeff's heart, especially when he terminated his extramarital relationship. Lots of counseling, prayer, and support from other Christians slowly brought healing to their broken marriage. Ten months after my first meeting with Jeff, I was praying with him and his wife as they stood at the altar to renew their marital vows. God had brought them both through an astounding process of reconciliation. Before family and friends, they testified to the power of the Scripture to change our lives for the better, by helping us to confront what is wrong and by teaching us to do what is right.

If we allow the Bible to equip us for living, we will often avoid the turmoil and suffering that comes from living without God's directions. For every man like Jeff I have known, there are a dozen others whose commitment to scriptural teaching has kept them from marital unfaithfulness. Sometimes they have been sorely tempted but rescued from devastating their families because God's truth lives within them. They have found for themselves that which the psalmist purposes before the Lord: "I have hidden your word in my heart, that I might not sin against you" (Ps. 119:11).

Sometimes, however, hiding God's Word in our hearts is not as simple as it sounds. The Bible is a large, complex, overwhelming book. Many Christians turn to the Scripture for direction in life, only to be confused by what they read or put off by the sheer volume of material.

As noted above, the Bible is the Word of God in human words, a divinely inspired but also human book. God speaks authoritatively through the words of people who seem to have lived "a long, long time ago in a galaxy far, far away," to swipe a phrase from *Star Wars*. God speaks distinctly but through many different and culturally distant voices. If we want the Bible to guide our lives, how can we rightly understand that which seems so foreign to us?

Reading the Bible in the Context of Intimate Fellowship

God has given us a means by which to understand the Bible: *koinōnia*, intimate fellowship. Bible reading is not something we do all by ourselves. Of course, at times we are physically alone when we read the Scripture. But, even then, God is with us, and God's people can help us though they are not physically present. The more we understand that Bible reading happens as an activity of Christian *koinōnia*, the more we will understand the Bible and be guided by it to grow in our relationship with God.

The Holy Spirit Helps Us Understand and Apply the Bible

We noted above that the Holy Spirit inspired those who wrote the Bible. This same Spirit helps us understand what has been written. The divine author is also our divine interpreter. According to Jesus, the Holy Spirit is "the Spirit of truth" who "leads us into all truth" (John 14:15–17, 26; 15:26). Most importantly, the Spirit teaches us about Jesus, helping us to grasp the meaning of his life, death, and resurrection (John 15:26).

For those of us who struggle at times to understand the Bible, how encouraging it is to know that we are not alone! The very Spirit who inspired the writers of Scripture resides within us to help us understand what they wrote.

The Holy Spirit gives us this assistance by helping us form thoughts that bring clarity to a passage we are trying to interpret. For me, Bible study is a genuine dialogue in which I keep asking the Spirit for guidance: "Lord, what does this word really mean?" or "What is the main point of this paragraph?" or "I really don't get this verse. I need your help."

Spiritual guidance does not preclude the hard work of Bible study, however. God rarely supplies definitive interpretation apart from the time-consuming disciplines of careful reading and research. Usually the Spirit's guidance happens imperceptibly as we examine a passage, using all of our human faculties and not simply relying on a spiritual zap to fill in the blanks. But, occasionally, the Spirit's help comes dramatically. At certain times, I have been wrestling with an extremely difficult passage. "Lord," I pray, "I just don't get this. You've got to help me." Then, all of a sudden, I see exactly what's happening in the passage, as the "wind" from God blows away my mental haze. Undoubtedly, my years of education and Bible study help me considerably when I am trying to understand a difficult text. Yet the Spirit assists all Christians, not only those who have a natural head start in biblical interpretation. When I talk with new believers about Bible passages they are studying, I am often impressed with the accuracy of their interpretations. The Holy Spirit can provide in a moment what it has taken me years of study to discern.

Of course, there are potential risks in our openness to this work of the Spirit. Sometimes Christians claim spiritual guidance for an interpretation of the Bible that turns out to be heretical. How can we feel confident in the Spirit's teaching if we could get it wrong? What is to prevent us from confusing our own creative but misleading interpretations with the genuine guidance of God?

We Help One Another Understand and Apply the Bible

Though internal guidance is an essential work of the Spirit, this does not exhaust the Spirit's contribution to our comprehension of the Bible. As we have already seen, the Holy Spirit places us within the community of God's people. When we interpret Scripture in fellowship with this community, we will hear God's Word more completely and truly.

In writing to the Colossians, Paul urges, "Let the word of Christ live richly among you, as you *teach and admonish each other* in all wisdom" (Col. 3:16 MDR). Besides reading the Bible alone, we need to place ourselves in relationship with other Christians where we participate in mutual instruction. The Spirit teaches us not only as we study by ourselves but also as we learn from our brothers and sisters in Christ.

Christian community provides an indispensable context for learning what the Bible means and for testing our own interpretations of Scripture. What we believe comes from the Spirit will be affirmed, or, if need be, corrected, by others when we share it with them (1 Thess. 5:21–22).

Within the church, certain individuals are recognized as teachers of the Bible because of their track record in biblical exposition. Usually they are people with special talent, education, and spiritual inspiration. Those of us who are identified as teachers should submit our interpretations to the broader leadership of the church. Even if we believe that the Bible is inerrant, we must remember that we are not. The very best biblical interpreters inevitably make mistakes.

Though each of us should study the Bible within a local community of Christians, we should also read the Scripture as part of the universal church of Jesus Christ. Responsible biblical interpretation happens as we share fellowship with God's people beyond our own community. Many Christians use study Bibles with notes prepared by scholars and pastors. When we read these notes, we are sharing in fellowship with believers beyond our local context. We might also find Bible commentaries to be helpful. The use of such commentaries connects our reading to the broader Christian community, often with scholars who lived decades or even centuries ago.

Face-to-face interaction with Christians who aren't just like us can also sharpen our insight into the Bible. Believers with different life experiences from us sometimes see things in Scripture that we overlook. Years ago I was discussing the meaning of Jesus' command "Love your enemies" (Matt. 5:44) with a Latin American man whose friends had been killed by the government because of their evangelical faith. This man struggled to love those who had murdered his fellow Christians in cold blood. He helped me to wrestle with the command of Jesus at a completely new level. Through this believer whose life experience was so different from mine, the Holy Spirit taught me something profound about the costly call of Jesus.

The Bible Helps Us Grow in Intimate Fellowship with God

Throughout this chapter, I have described the Bible as a set of directions for living. This analogy, however helpful, has limitations. Scripture is far more than a guide for assembling a workable life. It is also a master painting that gives us a transcendent vision of the living God. It is a symphony in which separate instruments playing unique parts blend together in perfect harmony. It is a personal invitation to an endless party. It is a collection of love letters in which God communicates his persistent passion for us.

If we read the Bible simply as a guide for abundant living, we will live better lives but miss the fullness of Christian *koinōnia*. It would be as if I received an anniversary card from my wife, Linda, read the card, and then decided to live in the knowledge that she loves me—without ever enjoying her love personally. I would be living truthfully, though skipping over the delight of a loving relationship. I would also miss the opportunity to grow more deeply in that relationship by embracing Linda and telling her just how much her card meant to me and how much I loved her also.

Many Christians use the Bible as a moral guidebook, a set of directions for right living. If they are careful in study and dutiful in application, they will tend to live abundantly. Yet, they will sense incompleteness in their Christian life. They will yearn for something more.

God has given us the Bible to guide our daily living and to guide us into deeper intimacy with him. Scripture reveals not only how to live by God's standards but also how to live in relationship with God. As each chapter of the Bible reveals new insights into God's nature, we learn to pray more honestly, to praise more energetically, to confess more freely, and to adore more wholeheartedly.

Each morning I try to spend some quiet moments letting the Scripture draw me into deeper fellowship with God. I do this by meditating on a relatively small portion of the Bible, no more than a chapter, sometimes less. In biblical meditation, I continue to use my intellectual faculties, thinking about the text and its meaning. But I also allow God's Word to penetrate my heart, to move my emotions, to quicken my will, and to influence every facet of my inner being. Sometimes I read a verse aloud, allowing each syllable to resonate. Sometimes I put myself into a story, imagining the feelings of the characters. Sometimes I reflect on the personal and theological implications of what I am reading. At all times, I try to be open to whatever the Holy Spirit wants to say to me.

Careful Bible study done in community with other Christians keeps us from confusing the genuine inspiration of the Spirit with our own biases. Scriptural meditation, done in times of quiet solitude, keeps our Bible study from becoming merely a source of theological data. When we unite the disciplines of study and meditation, when we allow the Bible to guide both our thinking and our worship, when we read both alone and in community, Scripture leads us into an ever-deepening relationship with the living God. Bible reading that happens in the context of *koinōnia* guides us into a deeper experience of that same *koinōnia*.

PRACTICAL QUESTIONS AND ANSWERS

1. "How can I get started in Bible reading?"

Commit to reading at least a chapter of the Bible each day. If you don't know where to start, Genesis is a good place. You might want to read the Gospel of Matthew as well. After you finish these two books, you might continue in order, reading Exodus and Mark. Or you might read a prophetic book and a letter of Paul. I encourage you to start with Micah or Philippians. A study Bible will help you understand difficult passages. To find a good study Bible, check with your pastor, your local Christian bookstore, or your Christian friends.

One of the best ways to read through the Bible is in partnership with others. Reading partners provide accountability, as well as a context to discuss what you are learning and what you find hard to understand.

2. "Which translation should I use?"

Some Christians argue vehemently for the superiority of their favorite translation. All translations, however, have advantages and disadvantages. I have used the New Living Translation for this book because it is very readable but still fairly accurate. I would urge you to use whichever translation is common to your church. For serious Bible study, it is always advisable to consult more than one translation.

3. "How can I learn to meditate on the Scripture?"

There are many different approaches to this discipline. All of them have in common the slow, reflective, prayerful reading of a relatively short passage of the Bible. For basic guidance in biblical meditation, consult Richard Foster, Celebration of Discipline: The Path to Spiritual Growth, 3d ed. *(San Francisco: HarperSanFrancisco, 1998). You might also find assistance in biblical meditation from the* NIV Worship Bible *(Grand Rapids: Zondervan, 2000).*

5
Intimate Fellowship and Prayer

When I was in college, everybody loved donuts. My room-mates and I would often make a late night "donut run," scur-rying over to the local Dunkin' Donuts to consume enough empty calories to keep our brains operating at full strength. Nothing contributed to academic achievement like a glazed donut with chocolate frosting!

Then we got older. Our waistlines got larger. The experts started warning us against those very ingredients that made donuts so delectable: sugar and fat. So we made a sacrificial switch to bagels. No more gratuitous sweetness. No more deep fat frying. Just a low-fat, low-calorie, low-pleasure bagel. (Of course, we could still destroy a bagel's benefits in a moment with gobs of cream cheese.) Bagel stores prolifer-ated everywhere as we left behind the follies of youth to pur-sue svelteness and lower cholesterol.

Then the experts spoke again. A bagel with cream cheese really isn't better than a donut, they explained. A piece of fruit and low-cal protein is what we really need for break-fast or late night academic achievement. But we got tired of the experts, and we still longed for donuts. So we started to eat them again. Donut consumption rose throughout America. Krispy Kremes became the watchword of a new breed of culinary hedonists. When a Krispy Kremes donut store opened near my home a few months ago, eager consumers had to wait in line for more than two hours to satisfy their yearning. After several months of donut gluttony, the lines continue. Meanwhile, bagel stores are closing like Christmas tree lots on December 26. Bagels are "out." Donuts are "in."

As with donuts, so with prayer. Prayer is "in" these days. Not too long ago, popular culture considered prayer to be outdated, like bell-bottom pants or flattop haircuts. The "in" people didn't pray, or, if they did, they didn't admit to it publicly. The world was believed to be nothing other than physical particles swirling around. If that's all there is, why bother to pray?

Yet, all of a sudden, popular culture "discovered" spirituality. Those who once spurned the existence of anything besides physical stuff started to wear crystals, explore Eastern meditation, and pray. Prayer became hot all over again, like bell-bottoms and flattops. The popularity of prayer, or at least something called "prayer," encouraged Christians to come out of the closet. All of a sudden, everybody was praying:

- Presidential and mayoral prayer breakfasts flourished.
- Athletes began praying publicly before their games.
- A recent Gallup survey found that over 90 percent of Americans claim to pray regularly, with 75 percent doing so each day.[1]
- My search of Amazon.com found 5,463 books with the word *pray* or *prayer* in the title. That could keep you busy reading for some time!
- Even the scientifically oriented medical community has shown an interest in prayer. Many credible studies dem-

onstrate that prayer contributes measurably to healing and health. Those who pray, or receive prayer, have fewer heart attacks and lower blood pressure, recover more quickly from illness or surgery, and need fewer antibiotics.[2]

All of this interest in prayer *seems* like good news for Christians. When we pay close attention to what people mean by the word *prayer,* however, the goodness fades from the news. Many who claim to pray do so in a generic, "define-it-however-you-wish" sense. Prayer is emptying your mind, or meditating on your dreams, or focusing on positive thoughts. One best-selling author explains:

> I don't pray to an entity. My thoughts are of being at home in the universe. If you don't think of the ultimate meaning of things as being separate from you, then there is no "other" to address. It's like fish trying to decide whether to relate to the ocean—they're in it.[3]

Certainly, this man is not alone in his love of "other-less" prayer, prayer without God.

Before we get swept along by the wave of popular euphoria for prayer, we must stop and ask: What is prayer? What does the Bible teach about prayer? Questions like these are not incidental but absolutely central to the life of faith. Prayer is not the donut of the Christian life but the main course of spiritual nutrition. Prayer is one of our greatest privileges, top priorities, and vigorous passions.

What Is Prayer?

Prayer is communication with God. When we pray, we talk to God. Prayer can surely open up a dialogue with the Lord, in which he speaks to our hearts through the Spirit.

But prayer is our part of the conversation. When we hear God's voice, we never say, "God just prayed to me."

Hundreds of texts from the Bible teach us how to pray. I have found one passage in Paul's letter to the Ephesians that neatly summarizes what we find throughout the Scriptures. This pregnant verse will give structure to our investigation of the nature of prayer:

> Through all prayer and requesting, pray at all times in the Spirit. And to this end, be alert in all perseverance and requesting on behalf of all the saints.
>
> Ephesians 6:18 MDR

First, we are to pray "through all prayer and requesting." In its simplest form, prayer is making requests of God. The idea of prayer as asking permeates the Bible, including the teaching of Jesus: "Keep on asking, and you will be given what you ask for. Keep on looking, and you will find. Keep on knocking, and the door will be opened" (Matt. 7:7).

The fact that Jesus urges us to ask in prayer disproves the contention that prayer should not involve requesting anything from God. Many spiritual gurus have asserted that, because God is all-knowing and all-powerful, we should never make a request in our prayers. Why would a sovereign God, they wonder, change his behavior because of our requests? Prayer, they conclude, really involves submission to God's will, not seeking divine favors according to our own will.

This view of prayer sounds very pious. It rightly recognizes the crowning sovereignty of God. It rebukes the petty selfishness that plagues some of our prayers. It underscores the submissive aspect of prayer, something we will consider later. But this view of prayer contradicts the basic teaching of Jesus, not to mention the rest of Scripture. Though we

79

cannot completely fathom God's ways, in his sovereignty God has chosen to listen to our prayers and to act in light of them. Through praying, we participate in God's work in the world. Undoubtedly, his ultimate purposes for creation do not depend on us. Yet in the unfathomable wisdom of God, he has chosen to respond to our prayers.

Jesus says that we are to ask *and to keep on asking* (Matt. 7:7). We should not stop praying just because we have asked for something one time. I have heard preachers actually condemn repetition in prayer. "If you pray for something once," they say, "then you should believe God and not pray for it again. To do so shows your lack of faith." Like the "don't ask" view of prayer, this too can sound pious, but it also opposes the plain teaching of Jesus (see also Luke 18:1–8).

Theology aside, we might balk at Jesus' teaching on prayer simply because we don't like being needy. We don't like having to ask for help. We'd rather be strong and self-sufficient. Prayer humbles us, reminding us that we depend on God for everything.

Praying with All Kinds of Prayer

Asking, though central to prayer, does not exhaust the content of our communication with God. According to Ephesians 6:18, we are to pray "through *all prayer* and requesting." All prayer includes giving thanks, praising, confessing sin, and offering worship to God.

Most of us are much better at asking God for help than giving God our thanks, praise, or confession. I have found this to be true throughout twenty years of leading prayer meetings. I often begin by suggesting that we offer praise and thanks to God for a few minutes before we lift up our requests. I'll model this sort of prayer with a few sentences that tell the Lord how wonderful he is. The person who follows immediately after me usually continues in the same direction. Soon, however, our declarations of God's glory become consumed by requests for divine help. One sentence thanking God will be followed by five sentences asking for hearts that are more thankful. We certainly need more gratitude, but sometimes our apparently humble prayers become ironically self-centered, focused on our inadequacy rather than God's excellence.

Offering all kinds of prayers to God does not imply that we should stop asking for what we need. Rather, we should seek balance in our divine communication. Many Christians have established a beneficial habit of preceding their requests with an extended time of thanksgiving, acknowledging God's faithful provision. As we allow the Spirit to remind us of God's good gifts, our heart wells up with overdue gratitude.

If you wish to grow in the breadth and depth of your communication with God, use the Old Testament Psalms. These 150 chapters overflow with a variety of prayers, including requests, complaints, praise, thanks, celebration, confession, and adoration. If you struggle to do more than make requests when you pray, reading and actually praying the Psalms can lead you into new avenues of expression.

Praying on Every Occasion

Ephesians 6:18 urges us to "pray *at all times* in the Spirit." Elsewhere, Paul speaks of praying "without ceasing" (Rom. 1:9; 1 Thess. 5:17). Of course, he does not envision the Christian life as one extended episode of heads-bowed, eyes-closed, hands-folded prayer. No one who lived such an active life as Paul could think this way. Rather, the encouragement to pray at all times underscores two basic principles of prayer.

First, every time is a good time to pray. The establishment of regular times for prayer helps to get us praying regularly.

Many Christians pray when they first get up, before meals, and at bedtime. They commit themselves to regular gatherings for corporate prayer. These prayerful routines provide a sure foundation for a life of unbroken communication with God. The divine conversation that begins in the stillness of morning continues throughout the hubbub of the day, providing a peaceful oasis in the midst of chaos.

Second, the command to pray at all times implies that prayer is more than verbal communication with God. At its simplest, prayer is talking with God. But as verbal prayer fills our lives, we begin to experience God's presence more regularly, even when we are focusing on something else, such as cooking dinner or returning phone calls. Prayerfulness of this sort becomes like a toddler's awareness of her mother. When my daughter Kara was young, she often played in the same room with my wife, seemingly unaware of Linda's presence. If Linda left the room, though, Kara's little antenna registered the change, and she would toddle off to find her mother. She lived in continuous relationship with Linda, receiving comfort and assurance from her even when they were not interacting directly. So it is in our prayerful relationship with God.

Praying with Alertness and Perseverance

Paul tells us to "be alert in all perseverance" when we pray (Eph. 6:18). The verb translated as "be alert" literally means "keep awake." As someone who falls asleep easily when I close my eyes, I have struggled at times to stay awake in prayer. In my youth this was a source of considerable guilt, because I would lose consciousness in junior high prayer meetings. How I wish I had heard the wise counsel of Dallas Willard, who once said to a bunch of pastors, "If you fall asleep when you're trying to pray, you probably need to sleep."

Years ago I discovered that, for whatever reason, it was hard for me to keep alert—not to mention awake—when I was sitting in a comfortable chair while praying. The classic kneeling posture kept me more attentive, but my bad knees soon distracted me with pain. Then I tried praying while walking. The results were astounding. I could pray attentively for much longer than I had ever been able to pray before. Once I got over the feeling that walking was somehow a less spiritual posture for prayer, I started walking and praying on a regular basis. The benefits for my relationship with God were striking.

In the process of giving myself the freedom to pray while walking, I learned a crucial lesson. Rather than fighting against every part of my physical existence, I began to work with my natural rhythms. I stopped condemning myself for my inborn inclinations and decided to work with them instead. I know many Christians whose daily relationship with God begins as they rise early to spend time in Bible reading and prayer. I know others who are simply not morning people. Even if they were to get up early enough to devote several minutes to the Lord, their devotions would be groggy. Their prayer life prospers when they set aside more wakeful minutes later in the day.

When Paul speaks of alertness, he means something more than physical wakefulness. Alert prayer involves attentiveness to the Holy Spirit, openness to divine guidance as we pray. I'll say more about this a little later.

In addition to keeping alert, we are to pray "in all perseverance" (Eph. 6:18). This means praying with intense effort. By implication, prayer can be hard work. It requires discipline and practice. It's not something we automatically master just because we've begun an intimate relationship with God.

You can easily get stuck in the quicksand of prayerlessness if you try to persevere all by yourself. God has placed us in fellowship with other people so that we might help one another to keep on praying. When exhaustion or discouragement makes it hard for me to pray, I find strength in the prayers of my brothers and sisters. As they intercede for me, I am empowered to bring my weary soul back into the loving embrace of our gracious God.

Praying for All the Saints

Paul exhorts us to pray "for all of the saints" (Eph. 6:18). A saint, biblically speaking, is not an extraordinary Christian but an ordinary believer. Every Christian is a saint, a person set apart by God for fellowship with him and for partnership in his ministry.

One of the central actions of prayer is intercession, praying for the needs of others. It is our privilege to bring our sisters and brothers before God's throne of grace, to ask for their healing, growth, and empowerment for ministry. Many Christians keep a prayer list to remind them of the people in their lives who need God's special help. When you go through a time of trial, nothing gives courage like the prayers of a friend.

Notice that Paul urges us to pray for "*all* of the saints." I don't think the Lord actually expects us to pray for hundreds of millions of Christians throughout the world. Nevertheless, the exhortation to pray for *all* of the saints challenges us to be aware of the needs of God's church beyond our own circle of relationships. It's pretty easy for me to pray for my family, my friends, and my church. I'm relatively faithful interceding for people with urgent needs. When I pray for folks in other countries, however, my heart is stretched. Every week in my church we pray for other saints, for churches in our community, for our partners in missions who serve Christ nearby and far away, and for the church of Jesus Christ throughout the world. These prayers affect God's activity in the world, and they also help us see ourselves from a fresh perspective. When we pray for Christians who are being persecuted in the Sudan, for example, our hearts become more tender and our passion for God's church more fervent.

Praying in the Spirit

Ephesians 6:18 invites us to pray "in the Spirit." The Holy Spirit, who was given to us when we first believed in Jesus, helps us to pray. Praying "in the Spirit" is not limited to one particular kind of prayer but comprises all varieties of communication with God.

When we pray with open hearts, the Holy Spirit guides us. Sometimes the Spirit shows us how to pray in a difficult situation. Sometimes a person comes to mind unexpectedly as the Spirit spurs us to pray for someone we would not have considered on our own.

Why Should We Pray?

Obedience to Scripture is a fine reason to pray. But there are many others. Jesus motivates us to pray by promising miraculous results:

> The truth is, you can go directly to the Father and ask him, and he will grant your request because you use my name. You haven't done this before. Ask, using my name, and you will receive, and you will have abundant joy.
>
> John 16:23–24

85

If we pray in the name of Jesus, God will give us what we ask. Now that's a good reason to pray!

God works wonders when people pray. Almost all Christians have at least one story of God's miraculous work. Those who pray faithfully have dozens or even hundreds.

Praying in Jesus' name is not a magic formula like "Open, Sesame." Although many Christians actually say "in Jesus' name" at the end of their prayers, there's no secret power in these words. To pray in Jesus' name means that we come before God in the authority of Jesus, not in our own authority, much as an ambassador of a king speaks in the name of the king, not in his own name. Furthermore, praying in Jesus' name also implies that we are praying for what Jesus himself authorizes (1 John 5:14–15).

We all know what it's like to pray for something that is outside of God's will. We pray, but the desired result doesn't happen. Usually we refer to this as "unanswered prayer." Actually, our prayers were answered. God said, "No!" We might not like it. We might not understand it. We might have thought we were truly praying according to God's will. But, for reasons we may never grasp this side of heaven, God said, "No!"

Jesus himself experienced God's "No!" in prayer. One of the most moving episodes in the gospels occurs just before Jesus' death (Mark 14:32–42). In a quiet garden, he falls on his face in prayer and asks his heavenly Father for permission to avoid crucifixion. "Abba, Father," he prays, "everything is possible for you. Please take this cup of suffering away from me. Yet I want your will, not mine" (Mark 14:36). But God says, "No!" God will not take the cup of suffering away from his Son, even though he prays repeatedly for reprieve.

This amazing story teaches us, on the one hand, that even the most earnest prayers offered by the most righteous people will sometimes get negative responses from God. If Jesus himself experienced a denied request, surely we can expect the same disappointment in our own lives. On the other hand, this incident shows us another crucial dimension of prayer. As we come before God's throne of grace with our bold requests, we are reminded of who sits on the throne—and who doesn't. Even as we pray boldly, we also submit ourselves to our sovereign God. Full-orbed prayer includes audacious asking and servile submission.

Prayer: A Path to Deeper *Koinōnia* with God

By scrutinizing the actions of Jesus in the garden, we come even closer to the heart of prayer. As we pray, God does what we ask when it's consistent with his will, and, more importantly, *we enter into deeper fellowship with God.* When God says "No!" to our requests and we are weighed down with disappointment, our laments keep us in touch with God. If we stop praying, or if we pray pretending that everything is hunky-dory with God, then our hearts withdraw from intimacy with God. The ultimate end of prayer, whether we are asking or complaining, adoring or confessing, is intimate fellowship with the living God. That's the best reason of all to pray.

Fifteen years ago, my father was dying of liver cancer. My family and I prayed for my dad's healing thousands of times. Prayer teams from the church laid hands on him and pleaded with God for healing. My father attended several healing conferences in which many people experienced dramatic miracles. Yet he wasn't healed.

I read and reread Bible verses that promise healing. I prayed with as much faith as I could muster. God said, "No!" As the relentlessness of my father's illness pummeled my soul, I began to lose confidence in God. Why would he not heal such a wonderful man, such a committed Christian servant?

One day after nursing my dad, I went out into the hills above my parents' home to walk and to pray. As I poured out my heart before God, I echoed the words of the Psalms: "Why do you remain so distant? Why do you ignore my cries for help? God, why won't you do something?" As I walked, the Lord began to speak to me in my spirit. First, for his own reasons, God was not going to heal my father's body. Second, God loved my family and he would not let us go. He had not abandoned me, my father, or my loved ones. On that path in the hills, I sensed God's presence, receiving the peace of God that is "far more wonderful than the human mind can understand" (Phil. 4:7).

God did not choose to take away my father's cancer. His ultimate healing came not in this life but as God snatched him away from death into eternal life. Yet, through my dad's suffering, God did an amazing work in his heart. My father was a decent, hard-working, obedient Christian. He served the Lord faithfully, mostly in ministry with children. The last ministry my dad performed before his death was as a counselor at a Billy Graham crusade, leading children to Christ.

But for all of his faithfulness to God, my father always manifested an awkward reticence in his relationship with God. He didn't particularly like worship services. It was hard for him to sing, so usually he didn't even try. He liked sermons but put up with the rest of the service. Yet, in the final years of his life, God healed my father of his fear of divine intimacy and expression in worship. Though we prayed for the Lord to touch my dad's body, God chose to heal his soul instead.

An image of my father is emblazoned on my memory. There he stands, his body wasting away from cancer, in the midst of a worship service that he once would have merely tolerated. Yet now he is utterly engaged in worship. My father, who never sang, is singing, and not just singing, but singing with gusto "I Exalt Thee, O Lord." He's standing, but not uncomfortably as he used to stand. No, he's standing energetically, hands raised to heaven. My reticent, hesitant, not particularly charismatic dad! My dad, rejoicing in God's presence with a freedom given only by the Holy Spirit. My dad, ready for heaven.

I still wish he hadn't gone there so soon. I wish God had healed his body and his soul. But I know that God never abandoned us. His ways are not our ways, to be sure, but his ways are always the best (Isa. 55:8–9).

Prayer puts us in touch with God's supreme love for us, a love demonstrated in Christ's death. When we pray, we experience the truth that "nothing in all creation will ever be able to separate us from the love of God that is revealed in Christ Jesus our Lord" (Rom. 8:39). Through prayer, we accept Jesus' invitation to make our home in his love (John 15:9). As we pray, we share intimate fellowship with a God whose love will never let us go.

Practical Questions and Answers

1. "If I'm not very familiar with prayer, how can I get started?"

The easiest way to start praying is to pray, simply, honestly, in a place where you can speak freely to God. Just talk to God. Don't worry about whether you're doing it right. Tell God what's on your mind. Lay before him your concerns. As you do this, open your heart to the possibility that the Holy Spirit might want to direct your prayers.

Let me urge you to pray the Psalms. Some psalms are not prayers in the literal sense, but many address God directly (Psalm 3, for example). You can read a psalm out loud, allowing the biblical words to become the words of your heart. Along the way, you might wish to pause, using the psalm as a jumping off point for your own spontaneous communication with God.

2. "When and how should I pray?"

There are no fixed rules. Even though many Christians devote several minutes to prayer early in the morning, you can't turn to a passage of Scripture that says you must pray every morning or that morning prayer is better than evening prayer. The Bible instructs us to pray without ceasing. As you grow toward such constancy in prayer, you will probably find it helpful to set aside certain times for regular prayer. I recommend that you begin and end your days talking with God. Be sure to thank him before you eat. One of these occasions for prayer could become a longer time for devotion and intercession. But don't get trapped in the dead-end way of thinking that you must pray for a long time for it to count. God listens to short prayers, such as the Lord's Prayer, for example.

Be sure to work with your natural rhythms. If you are a morning person, by all means get up a little earlier to spend some quality time with God. If mornings come way too early for you, set aside time later in the day. Try different postures of prayer: sitting, standing, kneeling, bowing, and walking. Some folks pray while jogging or lying facedown before God. In the Bible people tended to pray with their hands raised to God, but that's also not a fixed rule.

3. "How can I grow in my prayer life?"

Pardon me for sounding redundant, but the best way to grow in prayer is to pray. Remember that God has given us the gift of fellowship with other Christians to help us in prayer. One of the best ways to learn to pray is to join with believers who are good at praying. Most churches have prayer meetings or small groups that focus on prayer.

There are countless Christian books on prayer. Andrew Murray, With Christ in the School of Prayer *(New Kensington, Pa.: Whitaker House, 1985) is a classic favorite. Richard Foster,* Prayer: Finding the Heart's True Home *(San Francisco: HarperSanFrancisco, 1994) provides helpful guidance.*

6
Intimate Fellowship and Spiritual Guidance

Spiritual guidance is a marketable commodity these days. If you're willing to fork over a few bucks—sometimes, a few hundred—you can receive personal guidance from people who claim to have a special channel to "the spirit world." Many of these gurus hawk their supernatural wares at conferences and workshops. Others have turned to the Internet. Yes, you can visit web sites where, for a fee, you will receive personalized guidance from some immaterial being, an angel, or perhaps a departed relative.

Your "spirit guide" could even be a plastic doll. Barbara Bell, a forty-four-year-old quilt maker from Northern California, once operated the world's only Barbie channeling service. For three dollars, Bell summoned up the spirit of Barbie to solve the problems of those seeking her advice. "I appreciate and understand Barbie," Bell explains. "She has been forced to be shallow all these years, but underneath she's a profound person."[1] Frankly, I never realized there was anything underneath her slick plastic exterior!

All of this talk about spiritual guidance ought to give us pause as we begin this chapter. Sadly enough, some Christians have been caught in the current of spiritual absurdity, claiming to be led by the Holy Spirit into all sorts of nonsense. A man I knew once claimed that the Spirit had told him to fast, not from food, but from sleep. After several days of following the Spirit's directions, he could hardly walk without keeling over. Yet, in his stupor, he insisted that he was being guided by the Holy Spirit.

So, as we begin our consideration of spiritual guidance, let's do so with due caution, aware of our tendency to project our will, or even our own silliness, onto God. At the same time, let's not shrink back from one of the most precious aspects of the Christian life: divine guidance through the Holy Spirit.

The Holy Spirit as Our Guide

When we live in intimate fellowship with God and God's people, we will be guided supernaturally. Scripture abounds with examples. Abraham, Moses, David, and a multitude of Old Testament figures were led by God. In the New Testament, divine guidance comes explicitly through the agency of the Holy Spirit (Luke 4:1; Acts 4:31; 8:29, 39; 10:9–16, 44–45). The apostle Paul advises, "If we are living now by the Holy Spirit, let us follow the Holy Spirit's leading in every part of our lives" (Gal. 5:25). True spiritual guidance is Spirit-inspired. It comes neither from an angelic guide nor from a dead relative, nor even from the spirit of Barbie, but from the very Spirit of God who lives within us.

How, practically speaking, may we be guided by the Spirit? Are there certain experiences we should anticipate? Are there ways we might help ourselves to be more attuned to the Spirit? Scripture answers these crucial questions.

The Holy Spirit Guides Us through Circumstances

In Acts 16, Paul and his colleague Silas were guided through circumstances to a home in the city of Philippi. There they led a man and his family to become believers in Jesus (Acts 16:16–34). The ministry of Paul and Silas in Philippi didn't start off well. They quickly got in trouble with the Philippian authorities, who threw them into prison. There they met a jailer, who had no idea what was about to happen to him. Around midnight, when the two prisoners should have been bemoaning their fate, Paul and Silas were praising God. All of a sudden a great earthquake shook the prison, knocking the chains off the prisoners. The poor jailer, supposing that his prisoners had escaped, was about to fall on his sword when Paul shouted, "Don't do it! We are all here!" In shock, the jailer fell at the feet of the missionaries. He took them to his home, where he and his entire family were converted.

How were Paul and Silas guided to the jailer's home? The Spirit led them there by manipulating circumstances, some of which were obviously miraculous, others of which appeared on the surface to be quite ordinary. Stories like this one are common in Christian communities where people seek God's direction.

During my sophomore year of college, I had a fervent passion for telling people about Jesus. One Friday night I decided to wander about the Harvard campus to see if the Holy Spirit would direct me to a person with whom I could share the gospel. "Just show me someone who wants to talk about you, Lord," I prayed, "and give me an opening so I can get around my shyness."

As I strolled through the campus, no people in obvious spiritual need presented themselves. Nobody seemed to notice me at all. After walking around for an hour, I began to get discouraged. "Here I am, Lord, all ready for you. But nothing's happening. Why won't you bring somebody to me who wants to talk about you?"

Just then two attractive young women approached me. "We're not from around here, and we're trying to get to Dunster House. Do you know where it is?"

"It's a little tricky to get to Dunster House from here, so I'd be glad to escort you," I said.

As I accompanied them to Dunster House, I began asking questions with theological implications. No luck. For ten minutes, I kept fishing without even a nibble. These two women wanted to go to a party, not discuss religion with a stranger.

When I finally left them at the door of Dunster House, I felt supremely embarrassed, so glad that God alone knew how silly I had been. He was probably having a pretty good laugh on my account, I figured, as I began to slink back to my dorm.

At that moment I almost bumped into a student named Mike. We had met during our freshman year but weren't friends.

"Hey, aren't you Mark Roberts?" he asked.

Surprised that he remembered my name, I said, "Yes."

"You're exactly the person I need to talk to," Mike continued.

"Why?" I asked, mystified that this person I hardly knew would have any interest in talking to me.

"I've been meaning to call you for some time but just haven't got around to it. I've heard that you know about God. I need to talk with somebody about God. Would you be willing to come up to my room and talk with me?"

Never in Christian history has a wannabe evangelist found an easier point of entry into a conversation. As you can well imagine, I did indeed go to Mike's room, thrilled that my prayers had been answered. The conversation with Mike continued into the wee hours of the morning. We followed up with a weekly Bible study, looking at Jesus and his claim on our lives.

It's great to receive spiritual guidance through circumstances, but how can we be sure that our interpretation of our circumstances is correct? Suppose I had been so convinced that God wanted me to share my faith with the two young women on their way to the party that I managed to worm my way into the festivities, spending the whole night beating my head against the rock of their disinterest and thereby missing that providential meeting with Mike. Spiritual guidance through circumstances is great but usually ambiguous. What will help us to decode the circumstances of our lives so we can discern God's guidance with confidence?

The Holy Spirit Guides through the Bible

The Bible provides a reliable yardstick by which to measure all claims of spiritual inspiration. If, for example, you think the Spirit is leading you to do something the Bible prohibits, you can be sure that your spiritual lenses have become fogged. Throughout history, people have committed blatant sins under the claim of God's guidance. Their behavior contradicts the fact that the Spirit who inspired the writers of Scripture will never lead us to transgress the plain direction of Scripture.

Positively, if events in your life seem to point you in a certain direction, you can be more confident about that direction if it leads you to do that which Scripture affirms. There's no guarantee, of course. If you find a plane ticket to Indonesia, you probably shouldn't interpret that as proof that God wants you to become a missionary there. It's much more likely that God wants you to turn in the ticket so the rightful owner can use it. But, on the other hand, if events in your life give you an opportunity to share your faith with your neighbor, the fact that Scripture teaches you to do this very thing makes the probability of divine guidance more likely.

The Bible gives us much more than the ability to evaluate circumstances. It is the *primary source* for divine guidance in our life. As we saw in Chapter 4, the Spirit who inspired the biblical writers also works in our hearts to help us understand what God wants to say to us through the Bible. One of the chief functions of Scripture is to reveal God's will for our lives.

Often when folks say, "I am seeking God's will for my life," they refer to God's specific will, whether to marry a certain individual or to take a job offer. The Bible, however, usually refers to God's will in a more general sense, as that which all people should do. For example, "this is God's will, that you be fully set apart from this world to live for him, that you keep away from sexual immorality" (1 Thess. 4:3 MDR). If you are tempted with sexual sin, you really don't have to spend too much time wondering which partner God wants you to fornicate with. Scripture has made God's will abundantly clear: don't do it! Given the fact that there are thousands of imperatives in the Bible, we can't read too far without encountering divine guidance for our lives.

The Holy Spirit can also give specific direction as we encounter the text of the Scripture, taking that which is true for all Christians and applying it to our individual lives. This sort of thing happens all the time in personal Bible study, in group studies, and when God's Word is preached. You will recall the story of Jeff in Chapter 4. As he heard what Scripture says about marriage and divorce, the Holy Spirit spoke to his heart in a penetrating way, calling him to repent of his adultery and to begin repairing his marriage.

To one extent or another, we all read the Bible in light of our own presuppositions. We will tend to mold both the meaning of Scripture and the guidance of the Spirit to fit our own biases. Therefore, if we seek to discern God's guidance and not merely to project our own desires on God, our very way of thinking must be changed through our *koinōnia* with God and his people. As our minds are made new through the work of the Spirit, we are better equipped to determine God's specific will for us. This transformation is an ongoing process, something that begins in conversion and continues throughout our lives (Rom. 12:1–2). The Bible is the chief tool employed by the Spirit in this work of mental remodeling. The more we internalize God's Word, the more we will be able to determine God's will because our powers of discernment will be formed by the Holy Spirit.

But, as we saw in Chapter 4, God does not leave us alone to interpret the Bible in any way we please. Instead, he gives us the gift of Christian community, a place to find partners in the task of discerning divine guidance.

The Holy Spirit Guides through Community

Years ago two friends of mine informed me of their desire to marry. "We're not engaged yet," Ben and Sue explained, "because the elders of our church haven't considered our request yet."

"What request is that?" I queried. "A request to use the church for your wedding?"

"Oh, no!" they laughed. "In our church we have to get the permission of the elders in order to marry. We won't get married unless they give their blessing."

I was floored. At that time in my life, I could hardly imagine letting other people have such authority over a personal decision like this. But for Ben and Sue, it was a normal part of committed Christian fellowship.

As I look back on their situation, I can see the potential dangers in giving away so much personal freedom to a Christian community. Nevertheless, I am moved by Ben and Sue's willingness to submit such a personal matter to others for guidance.

Even those who have a deep knowledge of Scripture can misconstrue the Holy Spirit's guidance. However, when we join with other believers to seek divine guidance together, the odds of correct discernment increase exponentially. If you believe that the Holy Spirit is guiding you in some specific area of your life, you ought to submit your conviction to your Christian siblings. It's scary to do this, of course, because those around us are generally more open to God's will for our lives than we are, and they would be less likely to project our self-serving desires onto God than we would be.

Often the discernment of community can be an occasion for excitement as dear Christian friends seek God's guidance together. Several years ago my friend Neal, a businessman with a wife and two children, began to sense God's call to full-time, ordained ministry. He shared this feeling with his small group, which began praying with him for divine direction. One of the greatest hurdles Neal faced was his lack of seminary education. How would he be able to support his family while attending seminary? As he and his group prayed, they felt strongly that God was calling Neal to be a pastor, and therefore to attend seminary. So strong was their conviction that they pledged to help Neal pay for school and support his family. With their discernment and tangible support, Neal was able to complete his seminary education. He is now an ordained pastor.

The Holy Spirit Guides Us through Whispering in Our Hearts

Sometimes God thunders his will from heaven (Exod. 19:19). Usually he just whispers. We find a poignant example of divine whispering in the Old Testament Book of 1 Kings. As the story begins, Israel was languishing under the corrupt leadership of King Ahab and Queen Jezebel. The royal couple had led the nation to worship the pagan gods, Baal and Asherah. The king and queen had killed the prophets of God, replacing them with hundreds of pagan psychics. Only Elijah remained alive as God's true spokesman.

Elijah confronted King Ahab and his prophets, challenging them to a "my God is bigger than your god" kind of duel. Both sides would build altars on Mt. Carmel and prepare sacrifices on the altars. But they would not set fire to the sacrifices. Instead, they would wait for fire from heaven. Whichever deity consumed the sacrifice would be recognized as the true God.

The prophets of Baal went first, preparing a bull, placing it on their altar, and calling out to their god. When Baal failed to answer, they began dancing wildly around the altar, crying out for a miracle. But fire didn't fall. Baal was silent.

Then Elijah repaired the altar of the Lord that had been torn down by the pagans. He prepared his sacrifice and, just to raise the degree of difficulty for God, drenched everything with water. When all the preparations were completed, Elijah prayed simply, asking the Lord to demonstrate his sovereignty. God's response was stunning:

> Immediately the fire of the Lord flashed down from heaven and burned up the young bull, the wood, the stones, and the dust. It even licked up all the water in the ditch! And when the people saw it, they fell on their faces and cried out, "The Lord is God! The Lord is God!"

> 1 Kings 18:38–39

In the wake of victory, Elijah killed the vanquished prophets of Baal.

When Queen Jezebel heard what had happened, she sought Elijah's life, forcing him to flee to the wilderness. Several weeks later he found himself cowering in a desert cave, crying out to God for help. Then God instructed Elijah to stand outside of the cave and watch.

> And as Elijah stood there, the LORD passed by, and a mighty windstorm hit the mountain. It was such a terrible blast that the rocks were torn loose, but the LORD was not in the wind. After the wind there was an earthquake, but the LORD was not in the earthquake. And after the earthquake there was a fire, but the LORD was not in the fire. And after the fire there was the sound of a gentle whisper.
>
> 1 Kings 19:11–12

The God who had done such wonders on Mt. Carmel, the same God who controls the awesome power of wind, earthquake, and fire, chose to speak to Elijah through the "sound of a gentle whisper," what the King James Version calls "a still, small voice." The contrast between God's mighty power and his quiet voice couldn't be more stark. Though we might prefer dramatic demonstrations of divine guidance that knock us off our feet, the Holy Spirit often speaks in a gentle whisper that brushes our hearts like a spring breeze.

Unfortunately, a number of Christians today have trivialized this ministry of the Spirit. "God spoke to me" has become a virtual replacement for "I thought," except that by saying "God spoke to me" a person avoids having to take responsibility for his or her actions. We should avoid such language, unless we really mean what we say, because it takes the name of the Lord in vain.

While recognizing that the Spirit will speak to us, we must also acknowledge our tendency to misinterpret what we hear, or to mistake our own inner voice for the voice of God. Just because we think it doesn't mean God said it.

On the other hand, I've heard some Christians deny that the Spirit still speaks to our hearts in any direct way. This extreme view, however, opposes both the biblical record and the testimony of thousands of mature Christians who are not inclined to conjure up divine voices.

My friend Greg, a scholarly Presbyterian minister, had one such experience. One Sunday Greg was teaching an adult class in his church. In the midst of his lecture, a woman entered and sat in the back of the class. Greg, who had never seen her before, barely noticed her until he heard an inner voice say, "You are going to marry that woman." Not one to have such experiences, Greg just about fell over. Somehow he managed to finish his lesson. After class was over, Greg did not clobber this woman with his revelation but simply introduced himself to her. As their friendship developed, they both began to sense what Greg had "heard" on that fateful Sunday. Their brothers and sisters in Christ agreed that their relationship seemed destined for marriage. Finally, they did marry. Now, more than twenty years later, they have a wonderful life together. I suppose that a skeptic could chalk up Greg's experience to overactive libido. But, as one who knows his spiritual integrity, I believe that the Holy Spirit spoke to Greg's heart to accomplish God's will in his life.

Developing an Ear to Hear the Holy Spirit

In Greg's case the Holy Spirit almost shouted. Most of the time, however, the Spirit whispers to us as God did with Elijah. This presents an irksome problem: How can we hear the Spirit's voice when we are so overwhelmed by the cacophony of our busy lives?

As I write these words, I find myself in an environment that perfectly illustrates what I'm talking about. I'm sitting in a McDonald's Playplace, pounding away on my laptop computer while my daughter Kara races through a maze of giant plastic tubes and slides. Over-amplified Muzak fills this large, indoor room, but I can hardly hear it because of the competing racket from two nearby video games. Babies are crying; toddlers are squealing; parents are shouting threats as they try to get their children to leave the play structure.

Doesn't your heart sound just like this McDonald's Playplace sometimes? Have you ever sat down for a moment of quiet, only to notice that your mind keeps racing at breakneck speed? Do you ever try to hear the voice of the Spirit, only to be overwhelmed with dozens of other inner voices? It's no wonder that we find it hard to hear from the Lord, or that we mistakenly attribute some random thought to God. If we're going to be ready to hear the gentle whisper of the Spirit, somehow we have to quiet our hearts.

Throughout the centuries, Christians have found a way to internal quietness through the exercise of spiritual disciplines. These disciplines are exercises that help us get our spirits into good shape, even as physical exercise conditions our bodies. They are not works we do to earn God's grace but gracious gifts of God that help us experience deeper koinōnia with him. Worship, journaling, fasting, biblical meditation, silence, and solitude are among the disciplines that help us quiet our hearts so we can hear the quiet whisper of the Spirit.

As with every facet of the Christian life, learning to discern the voice of the Spirit is something we should do as a member of the Christian community. Certainly times of solitude are essential, but not a lifetime of separation from God's people. A healthy Christian community will help you listen to the whisper of the Spirit and discern God's own voice. It will also provide ways for you to grow in the exercise of spiritual disciplines.

Testing the Spirit's Guidance by Stepping Out in Faith

Sometimes we won't know for sure if we have correctly discerned the Spirit's voice until we step out in faith. This is surely the scariest part of spiritual guidance because it requires both trust in God and a willingness to be embarrassed. But, the rewards outweigh the risks.

Eva is one of the most mature Christians I have ever known. For many years she served within her church by calling visitors on the telephone. Usually she'd thank them for visiting and offer to answer any questions they might have. Most phone calls were short, pleasant, and appropriately superficial.

But, every now and then, Eva would "hear from the Lord." One time she called a visitor and began her friendly spiel. In the middle of her script, however, she sensed the Spirit speaking to her. For no apparent reason, she felt that this woman was in a great deal of pain over a difficult marriage.

After the pleasantries were over, Eva risked the embarrassment of following the Spirit's guidance. "Can I share something a little odd with you?" she asked the woman.

"I guess so," was the answer.

"Well, as we have been speaking, I keep having this feeling that you're going through a tough time in your marriage. You probably think I'm crazy, but I felt like I had to say something."

The woman on the other end of the line was silent for several seconds. Finally she choked out, "How, how did you know? That's really why I went to your church."

"I think the Lord told me," Eva answered, "so I can pray for you and help you."

Thus a friendly phone call turned into the beginning of a healing encounter. Eva's sensitivity to the Spirit, combined with boldness and gentle love, opened up an opportunity for ministry that might not have otherwise presented itself.

Spiritual Guidance: For Whose Benefit?

Eva's story illustrates another vital truth about spiritual guidance: It often comes not for our own benefit but for the benefit of others. Of course, as the Spirit enabled Eva to care profoundly for the woman on the phone, Eva herself felt gratitude well up in her own heart. To be used by God is one of life's greatest joys. But the guidance Eva received was not primarily for her own blessing but for the healing of another person who deeply needed to know God's love in the midst of a crisis.

Without a doubt, the Holy Spirit guides us through the maze of our lives if we seek his direction. Sometimes, however, we become so absorbed in seeking guidance for ourselves that we overlook one of the Spirit's main reasons for speaking to us: our ministry to others. When we are prepared to hear God's voice, we will often be led to care for the people God places in our lives. Sometimes the Spirit will lead us by placing a burden on our hearts for a certain person. Sometimes we will receive even more specific guidance, as Eva did during her phone call.

Spiritual guidance flourishes in the context of true *koinōnia* among God's people even as it enhances that *koinōnia*. As you are led through fellowship with the Spirit to care for others, your relationships will become deeper and more tender. The Lord will help you penetrate the guardedness that keeps us at a safe but superficial distance from one another.

Spiritual guidance comes not only for our good and for the good of others but ultimately for the good of God. The

Spirit guides us so that we might "do the good things [God] planned for us long ago" (Eph. 2:10). As we walk in God's will, God's purposes are being fulfilled through us. As my friend Buddy Owens says, "Guidance *from* God is also guidance *for* God."

When you pray, "O Lord, please show me your will," you are acknowledging that God has the right to direct your life. God is sovereign not only over all creation but also over you. We seek God's direction, however, because he is our Master and we are his servants, and because God's ways are the very best, both for him and for us. As we discover God's purpose for our lives, and as we walk in that purpose, he works for our own good (Rom. 8:28).

Moreover, we grow into deeper fellowship with him. Our *koinōnia* with God is the basis for our spiritual guidance. When we receive this guidance obediently, following as the Spirit leads, we draw even closer to God, experiencing new depth of intimate fellowship with him.

Practical Questions and Answers
1. "How can I learn to be guided by the Holy Spirit?"

Many people simply need to be aware of the different ways the Holy Spirit can guide them. For example, some who have studied the Bible for years to gain theological knowledge have never expected the Spirit to speak to them personally through Scripture. Once they have this expectation, they realize that the Spirit had been whispering in the past, but they had ignored this internal voice. Now they are ready to be guided by the Spirit in a more personal way.

Spiritual guidance must be evaluated for its consistency with Scripture. Moreover, we all need to be in close fellowship with other Christians who can help us discern God's directions for our lives. If you want to be guided by the Spirit and not simply claim

105

divine status for your own inclinations, commit yourself to Bible study and to active involvement in Christian community.

Finally, the practice of spiritual disciplines helps tune our ears to the voice of the Spirit. As you spend time meditating upon Scripture, praying, journaling, taking time to be alone with God, being silent for extended times, worshipping, and fasting, your heart will be prepared to hear God's voice. For wise counsel concerning these disciplines, you should read: Dallas Willard, The Spirit of the Disciplines (San Francisco: HarperSanFrancisco, 1988) and Richard Foster, A Celebration of Discipline: The Path to Spiritual Growth, 3d ed. (San Francisco: HarperSanFrancisco, 1998).

2. "My life is so busy, how can I find time to quiet my heart enough to hear the Spirit's gentle whisper?"

I imagine this question has been on the lips of many readers ever since I first mentioned our need to take time for quiet. Most of us live hopelessly busy lives, and when we have moments of potential quiet, we tend to fill those with lots of unnecessary noises. Quiet won't just happen magically for us. We need to plan for it. It needs to become a top priority in our calendars, or we'll be sure to find a lot of reasons to spend time doing other things.

7
Intimate Fellowship and Worship

Recently I ran into a man who used to be a member of my church. Jim left the church about a year ago, ostensibly because he and his wife moved several miles out of town. But I suspected that they had lost their enthusiasm for our church, though I didn't know why. The physical move had given them a gracious occasion to find another church, which they did right away, joining another congregation that was only a bit closer to their new home.

"So, how are things at your new church? Are you feeling at home there now?" I asked.

"Well," Jim began, looking embarrassed, "actually we're no longer going to that church. We liked the preaching and all, but after a while we just weren't getting those warm, fuzzy feelings in worship anymore. So now we've found a new church and we're really happy."

Jim's attitudes and actions are classic. They are rampant among North American Christians today, who understand the primary purpose of worship to be their own personal inspiration. What matters most in worship, we are led to believe, is our feelings, our experiences of elation, joy, and peace. Therefore, if we stop having warm, fuzzy feelings, like Jim, then it's time to find another place to worship, a place where gooey sentiments can flow freely once again.

But is the point of worship really to provide those who gather with a spiritual high? What is the purpose of worship, anyway? For that matter, what is worship?

The Essence of Worship

A passage in Paul's letter to the Ephesians helps us answer the question "What is worship?" This passage reveals the essence of worship and several biblical principles pertaining to worship:

> And do not get drunk with wine, which leads to recklessness, but keep on being filled with the Spirit, speaking among yourselves in psalms and hymns and spiritual songs, singing and making music to the Lord in your hearts, always giving thanks to God the Father for everything in the name of our Lord Jesus Christ, submitting to one another out of reverence for Christ.
>
> Ephesians 5:18–21 MDR

Although this passage doesn't use the word *worship,* it incorporates much of what Scripture associates with divine worship: psalms, hymns, spiritual songs, singing, making music, giving thanks, and reverence.

Notice carefully that we are to sing "to the Lord" in our hearts and give thanks "to God the Father." We worship in God's direction, for his glory and blessing. Though we might get warm fuzzies in the process, our worship is primarily for God.

The English word *worship* comes from an Old English verb that means "to offer worth" to someone. When we worship God, we acknowledge God's inestimable value and celebrate his unmatched greatness. Take Psalm 96, for example:

> Great is the LORD! He is most worthy of praise!
>> He is to be revered above all the gods.
> The gods of other nations are merely idols,
>> but the LORD made the heavens!
> Honor and majesty surround him;
>> strength and beauty are in his sanctuary
>
> Psalm 96:4–6

The primary biblical verbs for "worship," both in the Hebrew Old Testament and the Greek New Testament, emphasize another essential dimension of worship: our humble submission before God's majesty. Worship is like bowing to the ground before a king:

> Come, let us worship and bow down.
>> Let us kneel before the LORD our maker,
>> for he is our God.
> We are the people he watches over,
>> the sheep under his care.
>
> Psalm 95:6–7

Worship is communication with God, and therefore a kind of prayer. In worship we tell God how great he is, offering thanks and praise. In worship, we humbly offer ourselves to a God who cares for us like a good shepherd watches out for his sheep. We adore the God who loves us as a father loves his own children. In every case, our worship is a response to God, to who he is and to what he has done for us.

The fact that worship is primarily for God never occurred to Jim as he kept hopping around from church to church in search of inspiration. It's easy to understand how he became confused about the true purpose of worship. If you are regularly inspired in a worship service, you might also begin to assume that worship is primarily for you and secondarily for God. Moreover, the very structure of most worship services suggests that worship is primarily for the congregation, not for God. When we attend a service, we sit in the position of the audience, while the "players" act on what looks very much like a stage, even if it's called a chancel, platform, or altar. The primary actors offer a godly performance: singing songs, praying prayers, and preaching sermons. Though the congregation gets to participate every now and then, for the most part their participation focuses on paying for the show, that which we pastors call "the offering." No wonder so many worshippers think worship is for them.

When I came to Irvine Presbyterian Church, I was grateful for the legacy of our founding pastor, Ben Patterson. Ben counteracted the congregation's tendency to think of worship as something for themselves. To help them view worship in biblical terms, he borrowed an analogy from the Danish philosopher, Søren Kierkegaard. Kierkegaard spoke of worship as a play in which the normal roles were all mixed up. The congregation is not the audience but the actors in the drama. Worship leaders are prompters of congregational activity, more like directors than actors. God is the true audience. Worship is communication with God for his own pleasure and delight. Ben's foundational teaching about the true audience of worship has helped many in our church worship with authenticity by keeping their focus in the right place, on God and not on themselves.

Over the years, I have built on the foundation Ben laid with Kierkegaard's analogy, employing an additional image from Scripture that rounds out the metaphor of God as the audience. God is a heavenly Father, who loves us as his dear children (1 John 3:1). Therefore, God does not observe our worship in a distant way. He is not a picky audience that demands perfection or a heavenly drama critic who sits back to judge the show. Rather, God is like a doting parent watching his children in the school play (except that he doesn't have to watch through the tiny lens of a camcorder). To stretch the father-child image a bit further, when we worship God not only do we put on a performance for him but, as his children, we jump up into his lap and tell him how much we love him (Ps. 131:1–2). Worship is one of the most intimate forms of communication with God, an activity that lies at the heart of genuine *koinōnia*.

The fact that worship is *for* God suggests that much of our communication in worship should be addressed *to* God. Sometimes we get so wrapped up talking or singing about God in our services that we spend very little time actually addressing him. If we use the Psalms as our textbook for worship, then it is appropriate at times to address one another, the world, or even ourselves in a worship service (for example, Pss. 95:1; 98:4; 103:1). Nevertheless, worship that addresses God directly must not be overwhelmed by edifying words about God. For those who worship, and even for God, there is something uniquely meaningful about our singing, "I love you, Lord," instead of "I love the Lord."

When we forget to express our love to God, we are deprived of one of life's most profound experiences. But consider what God misses as well. As our heavenly Father, God delights in the love of his children. When we fail to adore him, God still loves us unceasingly, but his delight and joy are diminished by our lack of love for him.

It's always risky to suggest that God needs something from us. Theologies that make God dependent on us usually end up in the wastebasket of heresy. Yet some Christian thinkers have gone too far in the other direction, picturing God as never needing anything from anyone, an impervious deity who is fully self-contained and unmoved by humanity. This image flies in the face of one of the Bible's most astounding revelations. Jesus himself says:

> But the hour is coming, and is now here, when the true worshipers will worship the Father in spirit and truth, for the Father seeks such as these to worship him.
>
> John 4:23 NRSV

Isn't that amazing? God is seeking you to worship him! The God of creation wants to have *koinōnia* with you, to rejoice in you, and to delight in your worship. God does not need your worship because of any inherent deficiency in his nature. But the Lord has freely chosen to desire your worship, to be blessed by what you can give to him.

When I think of God as my heavenly Father, I can begin to understand the heart of God that delights in my worship. There's just about nothing in life that gives me more joy than when my children express their love to me. We celebrated Father's Day a few days ago. Among several expressions of love, I received a note from my son Nathan. I knew it was something special because he had been laboring over it for a long time. The note read:

> *Dear Dad,*
> *You are the best dad in the world and I love you very much.*
> *Over the 7 years of my life we had lots of fun and I dream in the future we will have even more fun.*
>
> *Love,*
> *Nathan*
>
> *P.S. Are you going to play Nanosaur today?*

This note still brings tears to my eyes and joy to my soul. Could it be that our communication of love to God moves his heart in this way? How mind-boggling to think that our expressions of worship can touch the tender heart of God!

Worship and the Fullness of the Spirit

Worship is our response to God, to his grace and love. But that's not to imply that we worship by our strength alone. Ephesians 5:18–21 reveals that our worship is inspired by the Holy Spirit, who helps us worship God.

Paul begins by encouraging us to keep on being filled with the Spirit (Eph. 5:18). This is not something we produce by our efforts but something God does in us as we are available to him. Though we receive the gift of the Spirit permanently when we first trust Christ, the filling of the Spirit is something that can and should happen many times throughout our lives.

This experience of the Spirit's fullness will flow into worship. As the Spirit permeates us, we will speak "in psalms and hymns and spiritual songs." We will "sing and make music to the Lord," always "giving thanks" to him. The association of the Spirit with worship echoes the teaching of Jesus: "For God is Spirit, so those who worship him must worship in spirit and in truth" (John 4:24). Worship happens in spirit, in our human spirits, and in the Spirit of God.

Worship is *a result of* being filled with the Spirit. As the Spirit fills you up, you can't help but overflow into expressions of praise to God. You will be like a woman who has just discovered that she is pregnant. Even if she tries to keep her pregnancy secret for a while, she inevitably breaks out with the good news. Pretty soon everybody rejoices over her secret because she just can't keep her fullness to herself.

Worship can also be *an occasion for* the filling of the Spirit. When we focus our minds on God, when we lift our praises before his throne, our hearts open to the Lord. In this posture of receptivity, we allow the Spirit to touch us, to heal us, to fill us afresh.

There is a reciprocal relationship between spiritual filling and worship. When the Spirit fills us, we can't help but worship. When we worship, we make ourselves available for the filling of the Spirit. Yet we must beware of thinking that our personal filling is the primary purpose of our worship. This perspective can keep us from understanding what we have already seen to be the most important truth about Christian worship: *Our worship is for God.* As we focus on God, however, offering praise, thanks, and ourselves to him, God often touches us, both supplying the feelings we associate with worship and, more importantly, pouring his Spirit into us once again.

Authentic Worship Involves the Whole Person

Worship is something that deserves our total participation. It involves our whole person, inside and out. Our text from Ephesians encourages us to make music to the Lord *in our hearts.* When the Bible speaks of the heart, it doesn't refer only to emotions but to the whole inner person, to what we call mind, emotions, and will. Thus Paul's counsel to "make music to the Lord in our hearts" echoes the introduction of Psalm 103: "Bless the LORD, O my soul: and *all that is within me,* bless his holy name" (Ps. 103:1 KJV, italics added).

We must remember the biblical sense of "heart" because of our postmodern tendency to reduce worship to an exclusively emotional experience. Worshipping God with our hearts includes feeling, to be sure, but also thinking and willing. God is looking for those who will worship him "in spirit and *in truth,*" truth grasped by our minds (John 4:24). If you can't seem to feel anything in a particular worship service, don't worry. This doesn't mean you aren't worshipping. You can still honor God by exercising your mind and your will to communicate praise to him. Remember, worship is primarily for God's glory, not your own.

Full biblical worship involves the use of our bodies in addition to our hearts. One of the most formative texts in the Old Testament called the Israelites to love God with all their being:

> "Hear, O Israel! The LORD is our God, the LORD alone. And you must love the LORD your God with all your heart, all your soul, and all your strength."
>
> Deuteronomy 6:4–5

Notice the last clause: *and all your strength*! How do we love God with our strength? By using our bodies to serve and to worship him. The Bible consistently calls us to worship God with bodily activity: clapping and shouting (Ps. 47:1), bowing and kneeling (Ps. 95:6), singing and playing instruments (Ps. 33:3), dancing and banging tambourines (Ps. 149:3), standing and lifting hands (Pss. 33:8; 63:4). Of course, we also use our bodies to serve God by obeying his commandments. Scripture assumes that which recent science has slowly come to affirm: We are not disembodied spirits living in a physical shell but a unified mind-body entity. Therefore, we will only fully worship God when we invest our whole selves in the process, both our hearts and our bodies.

Music Is Central to Spirit-Filled Worship

In almost every Christian community throughout the world, worship is expressed through music. This should come as no surprise. According to Paul, the fullness of the Spirit will spill over into music as we speak among ourselves in psalms and hymns and spiritual songs, singing and making music to the Lord (Eph. 5:19). Elsewhere, Scripture calls us to worship God musically. The Psalms call us again and again to "sing to the Lord" (Pss. 95:1; 96:1; 98:1). Psalm 150 urges us to use all the instruments at our disposal in praising God, including tambourines and loud clanging cymbals (Ps. 150:1–6). Scripture implies that music facilitates complete worship more effectively than any other human activity.

What do I mean by "complete worship"? On the one hand, complete worship happens when we invest our whole selves in praising God. Perhaps more than any other medium of communication, music facilitates total personal expression. When we sing, we use our minds, our hearts, and our bodies to devote all that we are to God.

On the other hand, music encourages complete worship because it fosters corporate worship. When I join with my brothers and sisters in song not only do I employ my whole person but I also join with them in unified expression to God. This was another reason to sing, according to the sixteenth-century theologian John Calvin: "[By singing in corporate worship to] the God whom we serve in one spirit and one faith, we glorify together as it were with one voice and one mouth."[1]

We must always seek to worship God with our brothers and sisters, a unified chorus singing "with one voice and one mouth." Though many contemporary Christians focus on their individual experience in worship, a "God and me encounter," the Bible commends corporate worship. Joining with other believers and worshipping God in unison with them is an absolutely essential aspect of biblical worship, every bit as important as our individual worship of God.

Singing "Psalms *and* Hymns *and* Spiritual Songs"

While we're on the subject of music in worship, we should notice the broad range of musical styles mentioned in Ephesians 5:19: "psalms and hymns and spiritual songs." We are to worship with psalms (probably the Old Testament psalms), hymns (carefully structured musical numbers), and spiritual songs (more spontaneous and simpler than hymns). Paul's instruction could be summarized thus: use a wide variety of musical styles in worship.

Many Christian communities have not heeded Paul's advice. The result has been impoverished worship, and, in some cases, divisive conflict. Churches could avoid this sort of conflict and enrich their worship simply by following Paul's counsel to use psalms *and* hymns *and* spiritual songs. In so doing, Christians would learn that different kinds of music have different strengths and weaknesses, and all kinds are useful for full-orbed Christian worship.

Praise songs are often (but not always) simple, and therefore easy to learn and emotionally engaging. Hymns are often (but not always) more complex, both lyrically and musically, and therefore more demanding, but also potentially more rewarding, both intellectually and emotionally. The eerie harmonies of chants draw us into the mystery of faith. Singing the Psalms helps us to join the chorus of God's people throughout the ages and to articulate our praise with the inspired words of Scripture.

Thanksgiving Primes Our Hearts for Worship

Whenever God's people gather to worship, they inevitably give thanks to God. We should not be surprised, therefore, that Paul emphasizes thanksgiving in our text. We should be "always giving thanks to God the Father for everything" (Eph.

5:20). Once again, Paul echoes one of the major themes of the Psalms, as represented in Psalm 92:1: "It is good to give thanks to the LORD, to sing praises to the Most High."

Thanksgiving is essential to worship for several reasons. It reminds us that our worship is our response to God, in which we act because of what he has done and who he is. God initiates worship by creating us, revealing himself to us, redeeming us, filling us with his Spirit, and continuing to bless us throughout our lives. Moreover, thanksgiving warms our hearts to the Lord as we remember his gracious works on our behalf. For this reason, expressing gratitude to God can be a helpful starting point for worship. When we "enter his gates with thanksgiving," we open our hearts, focusing on God and his goodness (Ps. 100:4). Of course, worship can take a multitude of forms, and there is no biblical requirement for beginning with any particular expression. But if you are struggling with worship, I encourage you to set aside an extended time for giving thanks to God.

Worship Impacts the Rest of Life

If we express our gratitude to God only in times of corporate worship, we miss Paul's point, because we are to give thanks "always" (Eph. 5:20). Thanksgiving and other expressions of worship should not be limited to official services but should saturate all of life. Christians seem to err on two extremes with respect to this instruction. Some, rightly arguing that they can worship alone, make a habit of missing corporate worship, thus cheating themselves, their church, and even the Lord—besides disobeying the biblical injunction to meet together with other Christians (Heb. 10:25). Others are faithful in attendance at worship services but neglect to glorify God during the 167 hours of the week they are not in church. Scripture calls us to join with our sisters and brothers for intentional corporate worship *and* to continue giving praise to God when we are alone.

Paul also implies that our worship will impact other aspects of living, not just what we label "worship." Being filled with the Spirit leads to *"speaking among yourselves* in psalms and hymns and spiritual songs" (Eph. 5:19 MDR). On the surface, this seems to be an odd statement. How do we speak among ourselves with musical compositions? Though songs, hymns, and spiritual songs are chiefly used for worship directed to the Lord, the more we allow these pieces to fill our hearts, the more they will influence our whole lives, including our speech.

Many believers testify to the way worship enriches their lives. When they feel overwhelmed, hymns of assurance calm their souls. When they are caring for a friend in need, just the right line from a praise song comes to mind. True worship permeates our lives as individuals and as a church. The worship experience of a Christian community affects every other aspect of its common life and ministry in the world. As we are being continually filled with the Holy Spirit, worship provides a channel by which the fullness in our hearts flows into our lives.

Worship Leads to Deeper Human *Koinōnia*

Although worship is primarily for God, it also draws us into deeper fellowship with one another. Praising God with other believers and humbling ourselves before his majesty foster deep human intimacy and unity.

Paul makes this point with language that might surprise us. As we are being filled with the Spirit, we worship in a variety of expressions, "submitting to one another out of reverence for Christ" (Eph. 5:21 MDR). Worship, it seems, leads to mutual submission among fellow Christians. Because the language of submission is emotionally charged these days, we can easily miss Paul's point. His instruction could be paraphrased in this way: follow the leadership of your brothers and sisters in Christ even as they follow yours. When we submit to one another, we acknowledge that our life is not our own private possession but an essential part of our community of faith. As brothers and sisters in Christ, we do not strive to dominate one another but to serve one another according to the example of Christ.

Worship prepares us to submit to one another, which can feel so foreign in our culture of autonomy. When we bow before God together, humbly subjecting ourselves to his overarching sovereignty, we will learn to trust one another enough to submit to one another. Our *koinōnia* deepens as we reject self-interest in favor of self-denial, placing the needs of others above our own (Phil. 2:1–4).

Arguments about worship styles in church are usually characterized by anything but mutual submission out of reverence for Christ. How sad it is that combatants in the so-called "worship wars" have disconnected what Paul so carefully weaves together: worship and mutual submission, worship and deep *koinōnia*.

Worship and the World

We have seen that worship is primarily for God. Secondarily, it is for the sake of the gathered fellowship of believers. In worship the Spirit is at work, healing broken hearts, inspiring faithful service, and building up the body of Christ (1 Corinthians 12–14).

But, from a biblical point of view, worship is also for the sake of those who are outside of *koinōnia*. Our expressions of worship, though addressed principally to God, are intended to communicate with and to draw outsiders into worship. We see this combination of intentions in the marvelous psalm of David in 1 Chronicles 16:

> Give thanks *to the* LORD and proclaim his greatness.
> *Let the whole world know* what he has done.
> Sing *to him;* yes, sing his praises.
> *Tell everyone* about his miracles. . . .
> Publish his glorious deeds *among the nations.*
> *Tell everyone* about the amazing things he does. . . .
> *O nations of the world,* recognize the LORD.
> Recognize that the LORD is glorious and strong.
> Give *to the* LORD the glory he deserves!
> Bring your offering and come to worship him.
> *Worship the Lord* in all his holy splendor.
> Let all the earth tremble before him. . . .
> *Tell all the nations* that the LORD is king.

1 Chronicles 16:8–9, 24, 28–31, italics added

Worship directed to God is also for the sake of the nations who need to bow before him. Notice that such "seeker sensitive" worship does not compromise God's majesty to make it easier for the nations to worship. God is proclaimed as "Lord" and "King," as the one who alone is "glorious and strong." The nations are invited to worship God on his terms, not on their own. Through genuine worship, we summon our neighbors to join us in *koinōnia* with the King of kings.

PRACTICAL QUESTIONS AND ANSWERS

1. "The idea of worship being primarily for God is a new one to me. How can I worship in a way that truly honors God?"

For many people, the knowledge that worship is primarily for God forever changes their experience of worship. You might need to remind yourself periodically of this idea, especially if it is new to you. At the beginning of each worship service I attend, I try to remember why I am present: for God and God's glory.

You might also try asking different questions after a worship service. Most of us tend to ask, "What did I get out of the service?" The prominence of this question assumes that my blessing is the main point. Much better questions would be, "What did God get out of my worship in that service? Did I worship God with all that I am, with my heart—mind, emotions, will—and my body?"

2. "How can I grow in my worship for God?"

Growth in worship comes primarily when we join with other Christians who truly worship God. If you want to grow in your worship, become a regular member of a worshipping fellowship, a church that understands the real audience of worship and structures its services for God's glory. If you are looking for a church, don't be overly concerned about stylistic issues. Instead, try to sense the heart of the church for God. I'd encourage you to meet with one of the pastors or the worship director and talk about the church's theology and practice of worship. On the foundation of corporate worship, you can also grow in your personal, private worship of God. I'd recommend The NIV Worship Bible *(Grand Rapids: Zondervan, 2000) as a helpful resource for development of your personal worship.*

8
Intimate Fellowship and the World

In the hit movie *The Truman Show,* Truman Burbank is a happy-go-lucky insurance salesman who lives in the perfectly manicured town of Seahaven, "the best place to live on earth," according to the headline of the local paper. It would seem to be so for Truman, his flawless wife, Meryl, his best friend, Marlon, and all of their sparkling neighbors.

As the movie begins, Truman goes about his daily routine, having no idea that everything around him is a farce. He is unaware that he lives on an elaborate stage set filled with professional actors. Even his wife and best friend are paid to costar in the wildly successful television hit, *The Truman Show.* Sweet, idealistic Truman is oblivious to the fact that he is the most famous man in the world, the star of a 24-hour-a-day, 365-days-a-year show about his life.

Living his apparently ordinary life, Truman never imagines that he is a special person, someone set apart by "the powers that be" for a particular purpose. He does not understand that he is fulfilling the vision of *The Truman Show*'s creator and producer, an enigmatic genius named Christof. His entire life has been dedicated to something far beyond Truman's wildest dreams, a fact that eludes his grasp until strange happenings finally begin to reveal the truth.

You and I are like Truman Burbank. I'm not suggesting that our lives are being televised to the world or that we live on a complex stage set. We are like Truman because we too have been set apart by "the powers that be" for a purpose far beyond what we might imagine. We too can go through life unaware of our specialness, never understanding that we have been designated to fulfill the vision of our creator and producer, the God of the universe.

If this comes as a bit of a surprise to you, you might be even more startled to learn the title that the Bible has given you to indicate your specialness. According to Scripture, you're a saint.

The Meaning of Our Sainthood

Typically, we use the word "saint" to describe some sort of super-Christian. From a scriptural perspective, however, all believers in Jesus are saints, without regard to their moral or spiritual achievements. The apostle Paul refers even to the Corinthians, who were snared by heresy and immorality, as "those who have been set apart in Christ Jesus, . . . called 'saints'" (1 Cor. 1:2 MDR). The Greek word translated as "saints" or "holy ones" refers to people who have been set apart by someone for some special purpose. They are "holy" because of their uncommon calling. We receive the title of saint because God has chosen us to belong to him and to do his work in the world. Sainthood is not receiving an honorary degree in Christ's kingdom but rather a letter of admission to his school of lifelong discipleship.

The metaphor of the school highlights another essential aspect of Christian sainthood. As a saint of God, you are one of many students in God's holy academy. In the Old Testament, God delivered the Israelites from Egypt to form them into a "special treasure . . . a kingdom of priests, my holy nation" (Exod. 19:5–6). In the New Testament, this same language describes our unique identity as Christians. We are "a kingdom of priests, God's holy nation, his very own possession" (1 Peter 2:9). As saints, therefore, we have been set apart from this world, but not from other Christians. As God's "holy ones" we are necessarily citizens of his holy nation.

We who believe in Jesus have been set apart from unbelievers and dedicated to a specific purpose, though, as we'll see, we are not separated from the world because the world is our arena. We fulfill our purpose in the world through *koinōnia* with other saints who share our calling. We are a holy people together.

Called to Active, Pervasive Holiness

The ultimate saint, the one who is uniquely set apart from creation, is God himself (Isa. 5:16). God's supreme holiness leads to a startling implication for us: "Now you must be holy in everything you do, just as God—who chose you to be his children—is holy. For he himself has said, 'You must be holy because I am holy'" (1 Peter 1:15–16, quoting Lev. 19:2). Our sainthood comprises not just our religious activities, not just our private lives, but *everything* we do.

Many of the activities we once routinely enjoyed actually compromise our sainthood by drawing us away from God. Consider Sunday mornings, for example. Most non-Christian people I know fill their first waking hours on Sunday with "doing nothing"—eating a leisurely breakfast, relaxing over the morning paper, or watching political talk shows.

125

None of these activities is particularly sinful. In fact, they sound pretty attractive! Yet even new believers in Jesus understand that their sainthood requires a change in Sunday morning behavior. They start attending worship services, often rising early enough to join an adult fellowship group as well. Sleeping in and lounging around in slippers become some of the old ways left behind by new saints. Even though we may still yearn for such leisurely moments, we must find time for them outside of Sunday mornings because we have committed ourselves to the "set-apart" disciplines of Christian community and celebration.

In the World, But Not of the World

As I mentioned before, Christian saints should not live in seclusion from the world. Unfortunately, some believers separate themselves from common folk, living in cloistered communities without any significant contact with the outside world. Others live in the world but sever all meaningful relationships with non-Christian people.

This isolationist version of holiness misses the distinctive call of Jesus. In the hours before his death, Jesus prayed for his followers, present and future (John 17:20). In this prayer, he recognizes that his disciples "are not part of this world any more than I am" (John 17:16). This will cause problems for them because the world will hate them even as it hated Jesus (John 17:14). Separation from the world, however, is not an option Jesus commends: "I'm not asking you to take them out of the world, but to keep them safe from the evil one" (John 17:15). In the classic phrase, we who believe in Jesus are to be "*in* the world, but *not of* the world."

Jesus prays that we will remain in the world, and he gives us a very particular role within it. We are the salt of the earth, those who preserve and enrich the goodness of this life. We are the light of the world, those who reflect divine truth into an otherwise gloomy existence. Our "good deeds" will reveal the glory of God to our neighbors (Matt. 5:13–16).

The Cost of Being a Misfit

Shining the light of God into the world sounds like a safe task, the sort of service for which one eventually receives the key to the city. But Jesus warns us that those who don't believe in him will "hate the light because they want to sin in the darkness" (John 3:20). Being the light of the world, therefore, turns out to be much riskier than it first appears.

Earlier I used Christian involvement in church on Sunday morning as an example of holy behavior. If you are faithful in church attendance, most of your nonbelieving friends won't worry about it much. You might be the target of jesting, perhaps pity, but probably not anger.

Consider, however, another situation that has become increasingly common today. What I said about leisurely Sunday mornings won't ring true for many people because they find themselves sitting not on their couches watching television but on hard bleachers as they watch their children play soccer or tennis. Sunday morning, once reserved for church-going or dilly-dallying, is now prime time for youth sports.

Many parents in my church have confronted the challenge of athletic events that conflict with church attendance. They have taken an unpopular stand out of commitment to the Lord. When one young soccer player was told by his coach to show up for a Sunday morning game, his parents, Jim and Donna, graciously told the coach that their son could not play on Sunday morning because of the family's commitment to church. The coach was miffed and tried to persuade Jim and Donna to change their mind. When they held firm, he made threats concerning their son's future in soccer. Undeterred, the boy's parents stood their ground. From that point on, their relationship with the coach was strained. He accused them of being "unsupportive." Other parents of boys on the team also were critical of Jim and Donna's "lack of commitment to the team." Even some Christian parents disapproved of their action. I have a suspicion that Jim and Donna, by putting Christ before soccer, shined a bit too much light into the lives of other Christians who preferred to live in the darkness.

Social conflict stemming from Christian holiness is nothing new. Many believers in New Testament times were criticized by "former friends" because the Christians stopped participating in "wicked things" with these associates (1 Peter 4:4). The spurned behaviors were probably pagan religious practices that permeated the ancient world. For example, if those living in the first-century Roman world wanted to go out with friends for a steak, they would go to the local pagan temple, the ancient equivalent of the modern steak house. Suppose, however, that new Christians who once hung out at the temple of Apollo realized that eating meat offered to idols in a pagan temple contradicted genuine fellowship with Jesus as Lord. What would their friends say? Some might dismiss the behavior as innocuous religious enthusiasm. Others would be hurt, even insulted. Genuine holiness often seems like "holier-than-thou-ness" no matter how humbly we try to explain our actions to others.

In some cases, the former friends of the Christians did more than express surprise. They also began to say evil things about their ex-comrades, accusing them of wrongdoing (1 Peter 2:12; 4:4). As a result, believers experienced social ostracism, perhaps even persecution. Yet God wanted them to continue their holy living even if it led to temporal distress (1 Peter 3:16–17). Suffering, as it turns out, is not an abnormal aspect of Christian living but something to which God calls those who follow Jesus (1 Peter 2:21). When we experience criticism, false accusations, or harassment because of our commitment to Christ, we should not be surprised. It's all a part of our Christian vocation. From God's point of view, we are saints; from the world's point of view, we are misfits, oddballs, even subversives.

Steve was on the fast track to success in his corporation. An executive with outstanding talent, he quickly climbed the ladder of success. Before long he was one of the corporate vice presidents, an up-and-comer touted for future greatness. Steve was also a Christian, a man who sought to live as a saint in every segment of his life, including his professional life. For a while, Steve's faith seemed to be an asset to his work because it supported his exceptional integrity.

Then Steve became friends with Ronald. Ronald also worked for the corporation, not as an executive, but as a custodian. Steve didn't see Ronald as a lackey, however, but as a human being and a brother in Christ. Casual interactions became deeper as they began to share their lives together. Their friendship was that of equals. Steve thought nothing of it when he began taking Ronald to lunch in the executive dining room, because all the vice presidents entertained personal friends there. But as soon as Steve started hosting Ronald for lunch, he noticed a subtle change in his work environment. Nobody said anything directly. Yet Steve's peers and superiors seemed dismissive of him and his ideas.

Finally, Steve confronted the company president with a direct question: "Why do I feel like an outsider around here? Have I done something wrong? Is there a problem with my work?"

His boss was honest. "No, there is nothing wrong with your job performance. But there's a problem with your atti-

129

tude, with your sense of company values. Frankly, bringing that janitor into the dining room just isn't acceptable."

Steve responded with equal frankness. "There's no rule that governs whom we host for lunch. We talk in this company about the value of all employees. I don't see what's wrong with having my friend join me for lunch every once in a while, even if he's a custodian for this firm."

"That is the problem," said the president. "You just don't see."

When Steve tried to explain how being a Christian led him to treat all people with dignity, he was told that his religious convictions belonged at home, not at work. End of conversation.

Before long, Steve was offered a different job in the company, far away from the main office and its executive dining room. Steve declined to move, primarily for family reasons. A few months later he was told to take a position at a distant location, or else. The message was clear: Steve was no longer welcome at the company. No matter what his performance had been, he had committed the unforgivable sin of seeing a custodian through the lens of sainthood and not through the prejudice of the corporation.

The details of this story may be unique, but the general themes are experienced repeatedly when Christians try to be saints of God at work. A woman I know lost her job when she wouldn't obey her boss's order to tell "a little white lie" in a business deal. A lawyer who tried to live according to God's priorities for his life started working less than the eighty-hour-a-week norm for his firm. Soon he was shunned as someone who "just isn't pulling his weight around here."

In America, we are blessed with an exceptional quality of religious freedom. We will not be incarcerated for worshipping God or publicly proclaiming the gospel. But if we dare question openly the values of the cultural elite, we will soon find ourselves the target of sustained verbal persecution. When a prominent leader, for example, publicly suggests that homosexual behavior is sinful, that person is attacked as a "hate-monger" and a "homophobic extremist." He is even accused of inciting hate crimes against gays and lesbians. When a Christian denomination makes a public commitment to evangelize Jews and Muslims, that denomination is denounced not only by media pundits but even by elected officials in official meetings of state and national legislatures. As Yale law professor Stephen Carter has demonstrated so persuasively in his book, *The Culture of Disbelief,* Christians in America who express their faith in public will be written off by the cultural elite, if not blacklisted for their religious convictions.[1]

Many Christians experience far more painful forms of suffering than being fired, shunned, or attacked in public. Throughout history and in many countries throughout the world today, Christians have been imprisoned, tortured, or killed for their faith. This very day believers in the Sudan are being sold into slavery because they are Christians. A Presbyterian pastor who serves a Vietnamese congregation near my church spent many years imprisoned in Vietnam because he dared to preach about Jesus.

Koinōnia with our persecuted Christian brothers and sisters will touch our hearts, both inspiring our prayers for their deliverance and moving us to work for their freedom. Moreover, knowing that thousands of Christians are standing up for Christ in the midst of severe persecution emboldens us to endure whatever suffering we might face.

Even if our suffering does not compare in harshness to that experienced by some of our spiritual siblings, we should expect to face adversity as we live holy lives in an unholy world. If we never experience difficulties because we are Christians, we are probably falling short in holiness or insu-

131

lating ourselves completely from the world into which Christ has sent us. Suffering is not an avoidable accident but an essential element of the genuine Christian life.

Suffering and Deeper *Koinōnia*

Whether it comes from religious persecution, social oppression, or natural causes, suffering can lead us into a deeper experience of Christian *koinōnia*. On the one hand, suffering forges more profound relationships among Christians. When one part of the body of Christ suffers, "all the parts suffer with it" (1 Cor. 12:26). If you've ever had the opportunity to share your suffering with those who have genuine sympathy, you know how this kind of sharing gives new depth to relationships.

On the other hand, suffering also can lead us into deeper intimacy with God. Certain kinds of pain help us feel God's heart in new ways. I once counseled a father whose teenage son had walked away from his faith into the perilous world of drug abuse. As this dad wept for his son, he shared what God was doing in his own spirit through this terrible experience. "I think I'm just beginning to know something about God's heart for us. I'm angry with my son for the wrong he has done. I want him to stop it. But, more than anything else, my heart is breaking for him. I would do anything to save my son. I would give up my very life for him." Indeed, this father was getting to know the heart of God, a God who in fact did *everything* for us through Jesus Christ.

When we hurt, God can seem very distant. Our prayers sometimes echo that of the psalmist: "O Lord, why do you stand so far away? Why do you hide when I need you the most?" (Ps. 10:1). But there's a wide chasm between our sense of God's apparent remoteness and the truth of his proximity. God does not stand far off, "watching us from a distance," as the popular song proclaims. On the contrary, our heavenly Father has drawn near to us in his Son. Jesus, the Word of God made flesh, entered fully into our humanity, even into our suffering, to help us (Heb. 2:17–18). Jesus knows our pain from personal experience. Even though he is fully God, he is able "to sympathize with our weaknesses, since he has been tempted in every way as we are, yet without sinning" (Heb. 4:15 MDR). Our triune God—the Father who loves us as his children, the Son who shares our humanness, and the Spirit who dwells within us—hurts when we hurt, agonizes with our agony, and never abandons us (Deut. 31:6–8; Heb. 13:5).

People of Hope in a Hurting World

In Romans 8, we encounter the good news of our new life in Christ: God, whom we address as "dear Father," has put his own Spirit within us (Rom. 8:1–16). But as we keep reading in this chapter, something hits us like a punch in the solar plexus: "And since we are [God's] children, we will share his treasures—for everything God gives to his Son, Christ, is ours, too. *But if we are to share his glory, we must also share his suffering*"(Rom. 8:17, italics added). Whoa! What is this? As believers in Jesus, we look forward to sharing in his own glory, but we must share in his suffering right now. This seems like more than we bargained for, both positively and negatively. The idea that someday we will be glorified along with Christ exceeds our expectations for heaven. The notion that we must suffer in the meantime, however, pours a bucket of icy water on our spiritual fire.

Why, if we are part of God's new creation in Christ, must we still suffer (2 Cor. 5:17)? Though we begin to share in the new creation the moment we believe in Jesus, we are still caught in the old creation for a while (Rom. 8:20–24). In this old world, we struggle as we look forward with hope to the day when "the kingdom of this world has become the kingdom of our Lord and of his Christ. And he shall reign forever and ever" (Rev. 11:15, translation from Handel's *Messiah*). We live in the tension between what theologians call "the already and the not yet." Christ has already died on the cross and rose from the grave, thus vanquishing sin and defeating death. We have already begun to experience the new creation through the Spirit. But the battle between God and Satan still rages, even though the final outcome is secure. We still struggle with our sinful and mortal flesh. Suffering is an inevitable component of our "in-between" status, as we live for God in a world that opposes him. Some suffering comes from the brokenness of creation, from disease, and natural disasters. Some suffering comes from the brokenness of human relationships. Some suffering comes from a world that hates us because of our allegiance to Christ (Matt. 24:9; John 15:18–21; 17:14).

Our life in Christ is like that of a woman who is nine months pregnant. In the last month of my wife's first pregnancy, she was extremely uncomfortable, carrying what looked like a giant pumpkin in her belly. Sleep came with great difficulty because no position would take away her discomfort. Yet as Linda suffered with physical struggles that would have turned me into a self-pitying lump, she abounded with hope. Joyfully, she counted the days until she would hold her baby.

That's exactly how we should live as Christians, with joyful hope in the midst of genuine suffering (1 Peter 1:6–9). We place our hope *in God,* in his ultimate victory through Christ (1 Peter 1:3–4). Hope that depends on what God has already done in Christ and focuses on what God will certainly do through Christ is a "living hope," a hope that will not disappoint us (Rom. 5:5). Christian hope is not a

Pollyanna-like naïveté about life, a simplistic affirmation that everything will turn out all right in the end. Surely, everything will turn out right in the end, if by "the end" we mean the time when God's kingdom is fully manifested. But, along the way, many things won't turn out as we'd like them to.

As I compose these words, a woman from my congregation is giving birth to her baby, a baby who died several days ago in her womb. My heart is heavy for this dear friend and her husband. I ache for the disappointment felt by their children. Their suffering is real. So is God's presence with them in their pain. They can have unfailing hope that God will be with them as they "walk through the valley of the shadow of death" (Ps. 23:4 KJV). Furthermore, they can be certain that, when someday they stand in the presence of Christ, their pain will have passed and their rejoicing will be complete. They can embrace the sure hope of the future, even as they endure the suffering of the present.

Enduring, realistic hope is elusive in our world today. From a merely human perspective, it makes no sense at all to be hopeful. If there is no God in heaven who cares about us, hope should be banished as happy-faced poppycock. Postmodern people have peered behind the veil of modernist hope in human achievement and discovered that there's nothing there. Cynicism makes sense in a godless world.

Christians are set apart from this world by being people of hope. Our holiness is seen in our hopefulness. We know what God has done, and we are confident in what God will do. Jesus says, "Here on earth you will have many trials and sorrows. But take heart, because I have overcome the world" (John 16:33). Jesus has conquered the fallen world and is in the process of completing what his death and resurrection began. Not even death, however painful it might be, can steal away our hope (1 Cor. 15:54–58).

"May the God of hope fill you with all joy and peace as you trust him, so that you may abound in hope by the power of the Holy Spirit!" (Rom. 15:13 MDR). May the Lord indeed fill us with this kind of holy hope—holy, because it is so unlike the world's despair, holy, because it comes from the Holy Spirit who dwells within us.

PRACTICAL QUESTIONS AND ANSWERS
1. "How can I begin to live as a saint?"

> *First, remember that your sainthood depends on what God has done, setting you apart for himself and his service through Christ. If you have trusted Christ for your salvation, you are a saint. So, be what you are!*

> *It might be that the Holy Spirit has already revealed to you an area of your life in need of transformation. Watch out for the natural tendency to rationalize away what God is saying to you! Instead, let the Scripture tell you the truth about your life. Ask the Lord for help in living by his standards, not the standards of the world.*

> *Also, remember that sainthood is not a solitary journey but a pilgrimage shared with other believers in Jesus. Commit yourself to a community of Christians who understand that they have been set apart by God for special purposes.*

2. "I feel caught between God's ways and the ways of this world. What can I do to live a holy life when it is so hard for me?"

> *You cannot live a holy life apart from the power of the Holy Spirit. God has given you his Spirit to help you live in a way that is different from the world. The more you spend time in koinōnia with God, the more you will be empowered to live distinctively. Bible reading, prayer, and worship contribute mightily to our active holiness.*

136

One of the ways the world reinforces its godless values is through peer pressure. If we are going to live in a way that displeases our secular peers and perhaps even causes them to turn against us, we need an alternative peer group. We need intimate communion with our brothers and sisters in Christ. Regular support, prayer, encouragement, and accountability will help us fend off the world's disapproval and delight in God's approval above all.

9
Intimate Fellowship and Our Mission in the World

In my early teenage years, nothing captured my imagination like the television classic *Mission: Impossible*. Intricate plots, dire situations, ingenious devices, split-second timing—all of these combined to keep me on the edge of my seat for sixty anxious minutes.

As the show began, Jim Phelps would play a tape that outlined some enemy plot crying out for immediate attention. Only Mr. Phelps and his organization, the Impossible Mission Force (IMF), could remedy the desperate situation. Their assignment was extremely perilous. Failure would be disastrous, both for the world and for the IMF. If a member of the IMF were to be caught, "the secretary will disavow any knowledge of your actions." The taped voice gave Mr. Phelps the opportunity to accept or to reject the impossible assignment. It concluded with those famous words: "This tape will self-destruct in five seconds." Its smoky demise led straight-away into the show's memorable theme music.

Mr. Phelps always accepted the assignment, gathered his team of experts, and, with unequaled skill, managed to defeat the forces of evil. The impossible mission turned out to be possible for the IMF, but just barely. Chalk up another one to human ingenuity and technological sophistication!

As human beings, we also face an impossible mission, but one that is truly beyond our potential. The problem: human sin and its results. The mission: to undo the dire effects of sin, to bring reconciliation between humanity and God, and to extend that reconciliation to all creation. The degree of difficulty: utterly impossible. No amount of human clever-ness or collection of spiritual gizmos will mend the breach between us and God and heal everything that is wrong with the world.

For limited and sinful creatures like us, overcoming sin and its results is indeed an impossible mission. "But with God everything is possible" (Matt. 19:26). God alone can fix what we have broken. God alone can reconcile us to him-self, and, as a result, bring reconciliation to a shattered world.

Yet, amazingly, we are members of God's Impossible Mis-sion Force. More accurately, we are part of his *Possible* Mis-sion Force. As believers in Jesus Christ, we have been drafted into the mission of God. To be sure, we cannot make rec-onciliation with God happen. That's God's job and he has accomplished it marvelously. Nevertheless, he has chosen us to be his agents of reconciliation who share in his mission of healing all creation (2 Cor. 5:18–21). Because we experience intimate fellowship with God, we are also partners with him in his worldwide mission.

What is God's mission? How does God accomplish that which is impossible for us? What should we do as members of God's mission force? These questions are answered throughout the Scripture, which, thank God, does not self-destruct five seconds after we hear it!

The Mission of God in the Old Testament

To understand our mission, better yet, *God's* mission through us, we must start with the Old Testament. God created human beings so that we might have *koinōnia* with him and serve as faithful managers of his creation (Genesis 1–2). God was to be the King and we were to be his royal family, those through whom he would implement his reign. Yet we sinned against God, rebelling against his rule over us. The result of our sinful rebellion was pervasive brokenness, in our relationship with God, with one another, and with creation itself (Genesis 3).

Only God can mend that which we have broken. That is exactly the mission he graciously adopts: to reconcile us to himself, to one another, and to bring reconciliation to all creation. Reconciliation restores the *koinōnia* that was broken through sin.

God begins to fulfill his mission by forming a special people—Israel—with whom he wishes to have intimate relationship as their king (Gen. 12:1–3; Exod. 19:3–6; 34:4–7; Judg. 8:23). But the Israelites reject God as king, and end up serving idols rather than the creator (1 Sam. 10:19; Ezek. 20:16). God uses the occasion of Israel's rebellion to make promises of future reconciliation. Some day he will save his chosen people from their sinfulness through a unique individual who will reestablish God's reign and extend divine reconciliation to the ends of the earth (Isa. 49:6). The prophet Isaiah speaks words that will one day fill the mouth of the promised redeemer:

> The Spirit of the Sovereign Lord is upon me, because the Lord has appointed me to bring good news to the poor. He has sent me to comfort the brokenhearted and to announce that captives will be released and prisoners will be freed. He has sent me to tell those who mourn that the time of the Lord's favor has come.
>
> Isaiah 61:1–2

In that favorable day, God will reign over his people, indeed, over all the earth. He will restore the gift of full *koinōnia* under his kingdom, a kingdom that will never end (Isa. 9:6–7; 52:7–10; Dan. 7:13–18).

The Mission of Jesus

Hundreds of years after Isaiah prophesied, another Jewish prophet emerged on the scene. Echoing Isaiah, Jesus of Nazareth proclaimed, "At last the time has come! . . . The Kingdom of God is near! Turn from your sins and believe this Good News!" (Mark 1:15).

One Sabbath day, Jesus went to the synagogue in his hometown. There he read the prophetic words of Isaiah 61: "The Spirit of the Lord is upon me. . . ." Following this reading, Jesus did a most exceptional thing. He announced that he was fulfilling this very prophecy. In effect, he said, "I am the one anointed by the Spirit to fulfill this prophecy of Isaiah. I am the long-expected redeemer of Israel. I have come to complete God's mission of reconciliation and to establish God's kingdom" (see Luke 4:16–21).

The passage Jesus read from Isaiah 61 highlights several essential features of Jesus' mission. *First of all, he was sent by God in the power of the Holy Spirit* (Luke 4:18). Even though Jesus is the divine Son of God, he is empowered by the Holy Spirit for his ministry (Luke 3:21–22; 4:1).

141

Second, he was sent to proclaim the good news (Luke 4:18). At the core of his earthly ministry was the proclamation of God's reign, that which would reconcile people to God and allow humankind to experience *koinōnia* once again (Mark 1:15).

Third, Jesus was sent to enact the good news. Jesus practiced what he preached, healing the sick, liberating the captives, loving the unlovely. He not only spoke of God's reign but also embodied that reign in his own person and ministry. Where Jesus was, there was the kingdom of God (Luke 17:21).

Fourth, Jesus was sent to form a community of the good news. When the poor, the blind, and the captives received the good news of God's kingdom, they had the opportunity to join the community of kingdom people. This community would live under God's reign, demonstrating divine love and justice (Mark 10:43–44; Luke 11:42; John 13:34–35).

Fifth, Jesus was sent to consummate the good news through his death and resurrection. Though he inaugurated God's reign on earth, human response to Jesus was limited by sin. He was sent, therefore, to proclaim and demonstrate the good news of God's reign, and to consummate that good news by overcoming the barrier of sin (Isa. 53:5–6; Mark 10:45). Because God's rightful reign over us was shattered by sin, the shattering of sin by the death and resurrection of Jesus enables us to be reconciled to God. Once reconciled, we can live in full fellowship with him as citizens of his kingdom. The cross of Christ invites us into the kingdom of God and restores our *koinōnia* with him.

Sent by Jesus to Continue His Mission

By dying on the cross for our sin and by rising from the dead in victory over sin, Jesus fully activates the good news. We can now be reconciled to God and live forever in unbroken fellowship with God. We can now begin to experience the new creation, even as we wait for the complete renewal still to come. Yet the once-never-to-be-repeated work of Jesus in dying and rising did not finish his ministry on earth. That ministry continues through the community of disciples whom Jesus sent to complete his work.

We who follow Jesus are a sent people, even as Jesus was sent into the world by his heavenly Father (Matt. 28:18–20; John 20:21). We are a community sent on a mission together: to keep on doing the ministry of Jesus so that all people and all creation might experience the reconciliation of God. God has designed the church of Jesus Christ to be a "missional" fellowship. The word "mission" comes from the Latin word *missio,* which means "having been sent." Individually and as God's people together, we have been sent to continue the ministry of Jesus, to proclaim and demonstrate the good news that God's reign has come through Jesus, and to invite people to be reconciled to God.[1]

Sent in the Power of the Spirit

If we take seriously our commission to do Christ's work on earth, our hearts should pound and our knees should knock. Given our manifest human limitations, not to mention our sinfulness, how can we do the work of the divine Son of God?

The risen Jesus instructed his first followers to *wait* before beginning their mission of spreading the good news (Luke 24:49). The disciples needed "power from heaven" and nothing less. Without God's own power given through the Holy Spirit, no one can successfully do God's work on earth. But, if you have put your trust in Jesus as Lord and Savior, you have already received the Holy Spirit. You have all the power you need to accomplish your mission. Unlike the first disciples in Jerusalem, you do not have to wait for anything. You have been empowered. You have been sent. You are ready to go.

Sent to Proclaim the Good News

The Holy Spirit empowers us to spread the gospel of God's reconciling work through Jesus (Acts 1:8). Though we do not imitate Jesus by literally dying on a cross and being resurrected, we give our lives to pass on the great news of Jesus' own death and resurrection and what these events mean for us.

The content of our good news is a revised version of Jesus' own message. Whereas he proclaimed the coming of God's kingdom, we bear witness to Jesus, to what God accomplished in the life, death, and resurrection of his Son. The language of the kingdom of God, so embedded within ancient Jewish culture, did not resonate well with non-Jewish people in the Roman world, the very people to whom Jesus sent his disciples. Soon the early Christians developed other ways to communicate the gospel so their hearers might understand. Rather than announce that the kingdom of God had come through Jesus, they proclaimed him as Savior and Lord. The salvation and sovereignty of God's kingdom was now expressed with emphasis on the salvation and sovereignty of Jesus. Same basic reality, just new language. This modified language retains its power in our world today.

Traditionally, Christians describe the task of sharing the good news by the word "evangelism," an English version of the Greek verb that means "to tell good news." But something gets lost in translation for many of us, because the word "evangelism" can fill us with dread rather than joy. The idea of "evangelizing" conjures up images that terrify many of us. We might picture Billy Graham preaching to crowded stadiums. Or we might envision a rainbow-haired man at the

Super Bowl, holding up a placard with "John 3:16" emblazoned on it. Or we might fear that sharing Christ with others requires us to approach strangers.

Unquestionably, God calls certain Christians to special ministries of evangelism. I am eternally grateful for the work of Billy Graham, whose preaching led me to faith in Christ. Yet I am not called to be Billy Graham and neither are you, I'd imagine. You and I are called, however, to tell the good news of Jesus in a way that reflects our talents, personalities, and spiritual endowments.

How shall we do this? It's much simpler and less scary than it might seem. Are you ready for the key to proclaiming the good news of Jesus? Here it is: *Just be honest.* Or, as my mother used to say to me, just be yourself. Talking with people about Jesus doesn't depend on your mastery of a sales pitch. In fact, the less you "sell" Jesus the better. As you honestly share your life, your convictions, even your doubts and fears, the good news will inevitably and naturally emerge.

I have learned two crucial truths about sharing the good news. First, our job is simply to be honest about what we believe and what we have experienced. God will use us beyond our expectations. Second, the Holy Spirit will help us in the process. If you start talking with folks about Jesus, sometimes you'll come up with an amazing answer to a hard question. But don't pat yourself on the back. You didn't make it up. It was a gift from God.

Sent to Enact the Good News

Like Jesus, we have been sent to enact the good news. We are to proclaim what Christ has done for us and live out that good news in our daily lives. We must speak of God's reconciliation and live as agents of reconciliation, as peacemakers in our combative world (Matt. 5:9; 2 Cor. 5:16–21).

We tell people that God loves them so much that he sent his Son to save them, and we love them with a divinely inspired love (John 3:16; Eph. 5:1–2). We proclaim the new order of God's kingdom and express that order by caring for the poor and seeking justice for the oppressed (Matt. 25:31–47; Luke 6:27; James 1:27; 1 John 3:17). We announce that Jesus has come to make us whole and enact that announcement through works of healing. The words and the works of the kingdom go together, in the ministry of Jesus and in the ministry he has sent us to do.

If Jesus had proclaimed the presence of God's kingdom, but had showed no evidence for his claim, he would have been rejected as one more religious charlatan. Yet by healing the sick, casting out demons, loving the outcasts, and feeding the hungry, Jesus showed that his message was true. Like Jesus, we must practice what we preach so that people around us will listen to what we say and perhaps even believe it.

Our world is filled with cynicism, especially about religion. We know too well the stories of hypocritical religious leaders, those whose works contradict their words. People are yearning for something authentic, not just more hype. The world will hear our good news about Jesus only if they see that good news enacted in our lives, individually and corporately.

We are called to live our faith as a demonstration of our message, not as a replacement for delivering it. Enactment alone won't communicate the good news of what God has done in Christ. If, for example, you are exceptionally kind at work, but never mention why, your colleagues will probably think you're an exceptionally kind human being. Who gets the glory? You do, not God! Only by *doing* and *telling* will people be able to praise God for his work in you.

How can we enact the good news in today's world so people might experience the presence of God and be drawn to

Jesus? In a nutshell, we are to do the works associated with God's kingdom. For example, even as Jesus healed the sick and sent his disciples to do the same, we have been sent into the world as agents of divine healing. This does not mean that you should set up your tent and hold healing crusades. But we can all be channels of God's healing power in manifold ways. For example, we can pray for the sick. By bringing people's physical ailments before God's throne of grace, we share in his healing work. Sometimes healings are immediate and astounding. Often they come more slowly. In some cases, God chooses to heal directly. Other times he works through doctors and medicine. And, of course, there are times when God chooses not to heal a person's physical body, but he chooses to do the greatest healing of all after he or she dies. Healing has always been closely associated with the mission of Jesus Christ, as Christians pray, as they use their medical abilities, or as they build hospitals and educate people about health.

Physical healing, however, is just one component of God's therapeutic work. The ministry of Jesus touches every part of our lives, not just our bodies and our eternal souls. Through the Holy Spirit, God heals minds, hearts, emotions, relationships, and even societies.

Consider the case of William Wilberforce. Born into wealth in 1759, he was known in his early years only for his love of socializing and his several physical infirmities. Wilberforce had no guiding purpose for his well-to-do yet meaningless existence. When he was elected to the British Parliament as a young man, he sought nothing more than his own fame.

But on Easter Sunday 1786, Wilberforce responded to hearing the good news and trusted Christ for salvation. Thereafter, he felt called to serve the Lord within government, and, ultimately, he focused his Christian energies on the abolition of slavery. Though discouraged by many religious leaders because of the impossibility of the mission, Wilberforce believed that God had sent him into politics to defeat the evils of slavery.

In 1788, he introduced a measure in the British Parliament to end the slave trade and was resoundly defeated. Similar measures were defeated in 1791, 1792, 1793, 1797, 1798, 1799, 1804, and 1805. Finally, in 1807, Parliament voted to abolish the slave trade, though leaving the institution of slavery untouched. For the next twenty-six years, Wilberforce continued his crusade. Finally, on July 26, 1833, the emancipation of slaves was ensured when a committee of the House of Commons ironed out the details of Wilberforce's bill. Three days later, after forty-five years of God-honoring effort, Wilberforce died, leaving an unsurpassed legacy of Christian concern for justice. His efforts encouraged American evangelicals who worked tirelessly for the abolition of slavery in the United States.[2]

Unfortunately, some Christians have driven a wedge between the proclamation of the good news and the enactment of that news, even though the Bible shows that Christ died *both* to reconcile us to God *and* to bring reconciliation among people (Eph. 2:1–18). By God's grace, however, the unbiblical breach between proclamation and enactment of the gospel has been mostly mended in our time. Many respected Christian organizations combine evangelism with social action, offering the fullness of healing as a demonstration of the gospel. World Vision leads the world in caring for and empowering the poor. Habitat for Humanity builds homes for the homeless in the name of Christ. Prison Fellowship seeks to lead inmates to Christ, to improve their treatment in prison, to care for their families during their incarceration, and to help them become contributing members of society after their release. Most churches invest their time, talent, and treasure in spreading the gospel and living the gospel through works of charity and justice.

You and I can enact the good news through our participation in some facet of Christ's ministry. We might visit shut-in senior citizens, or feed the hungry at a homeless shelter, or pound nails with Habitat for Humanity. Moreover, we can show our world the truth of the gospel by loving each person God brings into our path.

Sent as a Community of the Good News

When Jesus sent his first disciples into the world, he sent them as a community, not as a bunch of isolated individuals. How else would their mutual love prove to the world the genuineness of their discipleship? Likewise, Christ has sent you and me into the world, not alone, but as members of his church. We share together in the mission of the church, and the church shares in our personal mission. The same Spirit who empowers us for ministry is the one who immersed us in the church at the moment of our conversion so that we might engage in our mission as part of the sent people of God (1 Cor. 12:13).

Our corporate sending is so important because we get our training, encouragement, and support for mission from our Christian community. Here we learn what it means to have *koinōnia* with God and with one another. Here we learn how to live in a way that reflects the good news to the world.

Second, many aspects of the Christian mission cannot be accomplished by individuals working alone. You can probably tell your neighbors about Christ without help from other believers, but it's unlikely that you'll be able to evangelize a continent, or feed victims of famine, or build a hospital all by yourself. Yet, in partnership with other believers, you can do all of these things and more.

Third, we have been sent into the world together so that our corporate life will be a vivid demonstration of the gospel. God intends to show all creation his plan for cosmic reconciliation through the reconciled body of believers in Jesus (Eph. 3:9–11). In a world so filled with hatred, our mutual forgiveness announces the presence of God's reign. When people see our love for one another, they will see Jesus—assuming, of course, that we are in fact loving one another!

Needless to say, to be a part of God's sent people, you need to join with a community of Christians. Not only is your *koinōnia* with other believers necessary for your own discipleship but it will also draw nonbelievers to Jesus like a magnet. In a world fraught with alienation, a community of reconciled Christians shines like a searchlight on God's offer of reconciliation through Christ. Our fellowship together becomes the most important enactment of the good news. Through Jesus Christ, God has healed the breach caused by sin. He has reconciled us to himself and to one another, while entrusting to us the message of reconciliation. We are ambassadors of Christ together, sent into the world to deliver and to embody this good news (2 Cor. 5:16–21). "How beautiful on the mountains are the feet of those who bring good news of peace and salvation, the news that the God of Israel reigns!" (Isa. 52:7).

PRACTICAL QUESTIONS AND ANSWERS

1. "I could get pretty excited about being a part of God's mission in the world. But, frankly, I'm overwhelmed already. I've got way too much to do right now. What should I do?"

> *Involvement in the mission of Christ will alter our priorities. If we are going to invest our time and energy in God's work, we can't continue to do all of the other things we have been doing. We'll need to make new choices in light of new values.*

This process of reevaluation happens best in a community of Christians that is asking the same kinds of questions you are. In time, God will make his priorities for your life clear as you seek his will together with other believers.

Beware of the tendency, however, to get overly involved in worthy Christian causes without giving up other activities. Well-meaning believers can exhaust themselves by taking on more than God intends for them at one time.

2. "Even though you talk about 'just being honest,' I'm still not comfortable with the idea of sharing my faith with others. What would you suggest to help me get started?"

Let me suggest two quick answers to your question. First, find a person who is comfortable sharing the gospel with others. Spend time with that person. You will learn from what you see modeled. Moreover, you will soon realize that talking about Jesus with people doesn't have to feel strange.

Second, you might find it helpful to read one of the following books: Bill Hybels, Becoming a Contagious Christian *(Grand Rapids: Zondervan, 1996); Bill Bright,* Witnessing Without Fear: How to Share Your Faith with Confidence *(Nashville: Thomas Nelson, 1993).*

10
Intimate Fellowship and Transformed Living

As a child, I longed to jump off the high dive. I yearned for the joy of flight, the euphoria of momentary weightlessness. But I was also scared to death, afraid of vaulting into the unknown, afraid of the painful slap of the cold water so far down below. So, I would enviously watch other children as they enjoyed that which I both desired and feared.

After ages of angst, I finally got up the nerve to attempt an assault on the high board. I climbed the ladder and edged my way out onto the narrow board. When I finally stood at the end, peering down into the depths below, my body wouldn't move. I was petrified, literally. Trying to rev up enough courage to jump, I kept remembering the pain that was destined for me below. How I wished for the boldness to fling myself out into the void. Yet, at the same time, how I wished that I had never left the safety of solid ground. My heart was divided, split down the middle.

Do you know this desperate double-mindedness? Maybe it happens as you peer into the refrigerator, knowing that you should munch on those insipid carrot sticks as you ache for that fat-saturated piece of cheesecake. Perhaps your struggle comes when you have a bunch of tasks to complete before bedtime, but you can't keep yourself away from the latest episode of your favorite TV drama. Maybe you find your heart splitting in two when a part of you wants to hop up in the morning to spend time with the Lord, while the other part loves to wallow for a few more precious moments in your warm, indulgent bed.

Maybe your struggles are even more gut wrenching, with implications far more momentous. Though you love your wife and family, perhaps you are lured magnetically by a coworker who inflames your desire. Maybe you have always had an inviolable commitment to your marriage yet find your frustration with your husband driving you to the brink of divorce. Perhaps you have the chance to make a bundle of money in a business deal, but you realize that you'll have to compromise your integrity for the first time by "shading the truth." Or, maybe you feel your firm commitment to saving sex for marriage crumbling in the wake of your passion for your fiancé.

If none of these examples hits home for you, you can probably supply your own particulars, because we all go through the experience of internal division. We know what it feels like to be at odds with our own selves. Sometimes the toughest battle of life is moral solitaire.

The Battle between Flesh and Spirit

Most new Christians are delighted by newfound strength to overcome the sin in their lives. For the first time, they are empowered to do what they wish and to avoid what they hate.

153

Yet, as we continue in the Christian life, many of us find that our struggle with sin seems to intensify rather than diminish. Former temptations return to haunt us. Early victories over sin get mixed up with disheartening defeats. Often, with input from Scripture and the Spirit, we begin to recognize new areas of sin in our lives, behaviors, or attitudes we hadn't imagined to be wrong in our pre-Christian days of happy self-centeredness. The Christian life, that which once seemed to be a cakewalk of virtue, now feels like a marathon battle with vice. Though we want to glorify God in every part of our lives, we realize just how much we live instead for our own glory and pleasure. At times we feel completely helpless to make things better. Our hearts echo the lament of Paul in Romans 7:

> I don't understand myself at all, for I really want to do what is right, but I don't do it. Instead, I do the very thing I hate. . . . No matter which way I turn, I can't make myself do right. I want to, but I can't. When I want to do good, I don't. And when I try not to do wrong, I do it anyway.
>
> Romans 7:15–19

Sound familiar?

The Bible describes this internal wrestling match as a battle between flesh and Spirit (Gal. 5:17). Even though we have received the Holy Spirit, our flesh, the part of us that is sinful and resistant to God, has not been obliterated. We desire that which stands opposed to God, even though the Spirit within us desires that which honors God. We are caught in a struggle not simply between our own flesh and our own spirit but between our flesh and the Spirit of God. When we give way to the desires of our sinful flesh, we produce the "works of the flesh":

154

. . . sexual immorality, impure thoughts, eagerness of lustful pleasure, idolatry, participation in demonic activities, hostility, quarreling, jealousy, outbursts of anger, selfish ambition, divisions, the feeling that everyone is wrong except those in your own little group, envy, drunkenness, wild parties, and other kinds of sin.

Galatians 5:19–21

Though we tend to limit "fleshly" sins to those that involve our physical bodies directly, things like sexual immorality or drunkenness, from a biblical point of view, every human sin is a work of our flesh.

Aren't We Already Holy?

"But," you might wonder, "haven't we become a part of God's new creation at the moment of our conversion? Haven't we been declared holy by God? Doesn't the Holy Spirit live in us? How can our life be a battle between our sinful flesh and the Spirit?"

To be sure, "those who become Christians become new persons. They are not the same anymore, for the old life is gone. A new life has begun!" (2 Cor. 5:17). As an essential component of this new life, God makes us holy, setting us apart for his purposes and giving us the Holy Spirit. Yet, as we saw in chapter 8, we live in the tension between the "already and the not yet." We already live as transformed people but are not yet perfected. We already experience forgiveness for our sin but have not completely stopped sinning. We have already been set apart as God's holy people but do not live altogether holy lives. We have already received the indwelling Holy Spirit, yet we have not fully yielded ourselves to the Spirit's influence. Centuries ago, British theologians recognized that, though God has begun the work of making us fully holy, there remain in us "some remnants of corruption in every part, whence arises *a continual and irreconcilable war,* the flesh lusting against the Spirit, and the Spirit against the flesh."[1]

Ironically, as we grow in our faith, we tend to see our sinfulness more clearly and despise our "flesh" more vehemently. That in which we once delighted now becomes a source of shame as we "do the very thing we hate," to use Paul's language from Romans 7. We end up a bit like Lemuel Gulliver in Jonathan Swift's classic satire, *Gulliver's Travels.*[2] After a series of journeys to strange civilizations throughout the world, Gulliver ends up in the land of the Houyhnhnms. The Houyhnhnms are horses who are endowed with speech, intelligence, and wisdom. They exemplify the qualities we associate with human excellence. The land of the Houyhnhnms is also inhabited by the Yahoos. These beings are human but gross examples of all that is despicable in human nature. They live as inarticulate brutes, groveling in their bestial nature. In his effort to make human existence more palatable to the Houyhnhnms, Gulliver recounts the virtues of European civilization. Yet, honesty forces him to chronicle the manifold evils of the human race. The more he endeavors to defend humankind, the more he reveals our vile, "fleshly" nature. Though we have the use of reason and language, our moral character looks just as disgusting as that of the coarse, brutish Yahoos. After spending several years with the honorable Houyhnhnms, Gulliver sees his human nature from a completely different perspective. He comes to despise himself and all other persons as mere Yahoos. When he finally returns to his home in England, he can't stand to be in the same room with people, even his own wife and children.

Sometimes I feel like a Yahoo. I get so tired of my own sinfulness that I don't want to remain in the same room with myself! Have you ever known that feeling? Have you ever done the very thing that you hate? At times, our sinful nature keeps hounding us like a guard dog pursuing a trespasser. Temptation from within combines with temptations all around, and we sink into the quicksand of sin. Our souls echo the lament of Paul: "Oh, what a miserable person I am! Who will free me from this life that is dominated by sin?" (Rom. 7:24).

The Limits of Legalism

Surely the Holy Spirit has not shown us our sin to let us flounder in the muck of self-hatred. When we feel sickened by our sin, we rightly sense that God intends so much better for us. Some of us, therefore, resolve to improve our behavior and to transform our sinful flesh. We fill our lives with lots of do's and don'ts, trying to hedge ourselves in so that we have no choice other than to behave properly. We live according to law, adopting a moral posture theologians describe as "legalism."

But there's an inherent flaw in legalism. Even if we choose the right code for our lives—the Ten Commandments, for example—we find that we cannot live according to that code, no matter how hard we try. Our sinful nature keeps us from doing that which we know to be right, no matter how clever we may be.

We end up like my friend James, who wanted to get up each morning for a quiet time with God but stumbled over his own sleepiness. At first he set his alarm clock for a sufficiently early hour, but he'd simply hit the snooze button. Then he set the clock on the other side of the room, taking away the option of quieting the alarm without getting out of bed. Before too long, however, he learned to cross the room, turn off the alarm, and return to his inviting bed—all without opening his eyes. Then James bought another clock and put it in his living room, setting this clock a few minutes later than the one on the other side of his room. Maybe if he had to trek all the way into the next room, James figured, he would be awake enough to stay up for a few moments with God. But, alas, this didn't work either. At that point, he actually considered locking his clock in some sort of cage, thus forcing himself to wake up enough to turn a padlock to the right numbers. Sadly, he realized that he could easily unplug the clock. James was stumped. He just wasn't going to wake up early enough to get in a quiet time at the beginning of the day.

You might wonder why James didn't go to bed earlier. A good question, indeed! It points to the fatal flaw in legalism. No matter how hard we try to force ourselves by rules to do what is right or to avoid what is wrong, we inevitably fail because we don't have the moral strength to succeed. Failed diets, abandoned New Year's resolutions, and discarded to-do lists—all these testify to our inherent moral limitations.

Any system of rights and wrongs, even if it's God's revealed law, turns out to be inadequate for behavioral transformation. In fact, divine law magnifies our failures. According to Paul, "the more we know God's law, the clearer it becomes that we aren't obeying it" (Rom. 3:20). Even as living by the law can't bring us into restored relationship with God, so it can't lead to transformed living.

Keep Walking in the Spirit!

Paul provides the key to behavioral transformation in his letter to the Galatians. Like many of us, the Christians in Galatia had attempted to turn the Christian life into a legalistic endeavor, with dire results. So, after showing how legalism is inconsistent with the grace of God in Christ, Paul writes: "So I tell you, keep on walking in the Spirit and you will not fulfill the desire of the flesh" (Gal. 5:16 MDR). The Greek original of this verse accentuates the cause and effect relationship between the clauses: "Keep on walking in the Spirit *and you will not* fulfill the desire of the flesh" (italics added). Walking in the Spirit is the key with which we lock up the desire of our sinful nature.

"To walk in the Spirit" is to live each day in fellowship with the Holy Spirit. Living in relationship with the Spirit isn't something you do every now and then. It's a daily experience of God's presence and power. And this experience will strengthen you to overcome your sinful flesh.

This is great news! You are not doomed to a life of Yahoo-like baseness. You are not mired forever in sin. If you walk each day in the Spirit, you will find the ability to stop fulfilling your sinful desires. You will experience victory in the fundamental battle of your life.

If you are feeling defeated by sin right now, remember: The power to overcome the flesh is in you through the Holy Spirit. If you wish to access that power, you must seek deeper and more regular *koinōnia* with the Spirit. As I write this chapter, I have been a Christian for thirty-seven years. During this span of time, I have struggled with my sinful nature, living daily in the battle between flesh and Spirit. If God had assigned an angel to keep score of my sins (which, thank God, has not happened!), and if he allowed you to read the scorecard (which, thank God, will not happen!), you'd find an interesting pattern in my sinfulness. When I fail to spend time with God, I quickly add to my sordid collection of sins. But when I devote more time to *koinōnia* with God, I sin less. Furthermore, as I grow in relationship with God through the Spirit, my heart and my lifestyle are more thoroughly transformed. Walking in the Spirit empowers me to avoid sin and to live rightly.

159

The Fruit of the Spirit

After urging us to keep on living in the Spirit so that we might achieve victory over our flesh, Paul goes on to describe positively what will happen in our lives if we do this: "But when the Holy Spirit controls our lives, he will produce this kind of fruit in us: love, joy, peace, patience, kindness, goodness, faithfulness, gentleness, and self-control" (Gal. 5:22–23). We don't produce fruit by our efforts, even as an apple tree doesn't toil to grow apples. Rather, fruit grows automatically as the tree sends its roots into fertile soil. Likewise, we will produce divine fruit when our roots grow deeply into the Holy Spirit.

Notice that spiritual fruit cannot grow unless we are also in relationship with others, in actual *koinōnia* with other people. Love, patience, kindness, and gentleness, key aspects of the fruit of the Spirit, cannot exist outside of human relationships. We will be transformed more fully by the Spirit when we commit ourselves to the fullness of Christian *koinōnia*.

Saved *for* Good Works

Are good works necessary to the Christian life? How much emphasis should we place on doing good works? Questions like these have challenged Christians since the first century. The debate reached a climax in the sixteenth century when Protestant Christians split from the Roman Catholic Church, in part over the role of good works in salvation. To put the matter simply, Protestants insisted that we are saved by grace alone through faith alone, while Catholics stressed the importance of good works as a part of our contribution to salvation. In recent years, the theological divide between Protestantism and Catholicism has narrowed considerably, but in previous centuries it was vast, and sometimes the cause for vicious fighting among Christians.

I felt a bit of that history sneak up on me a couple of years ago when I was the Protestant representative on a panel that included a Catholic priest and a Greek Orthodox priest. We were explaining to the audience the similarities and differences between our understandings of the Christian life. I was articulating the Protestant commitment to salvation "by grace through faith," referring to Ephesians 2:8, when a member of the audience interrupted me with a question.

"What about good works?" he blurted out. "How can you talk about salvation without mentioning good works? You are saying that works don't matter!"

Actually, he interrupted me right before I would have addressed his point. Paul's insistence that we are "saved by grace through faith" in Ephesians 2:8 flows into his additional comment: "For we are what [God] has made us, *created in Christ Jesus for good works,* which God prepared beforehand to be our way of life" (Eph. 2:10 NRSV, italics added). Though we are saved by grace through faith, *not by works,* we are nevertheless newly created in Christ *for good works.* Good works, therefore, are an essential component of the whole salvation scheme. They do not cause us to be saved, but they necessarily follow from our salvation.

If you claim to be saved by grace through faith in Jesus, yet there is no evidence of good works in your life, then your claim becomes suspect. Either you have not really trusted in Jesus, or you have taken the first step but fallen immediately into a life of sin. When salvation is genuine, transformation will follow and good works will be produced.

Human *Koinōnia* and Transformed Living

From Galatians 5 we learn that we are transformed by the Holy Spirit, enabled to deny our fleshly desires, and blessed with the fruit of the Spirit. *Koinōnia* with the Spirit is the

161

essential power behind this transformation. I already mentioned that spiritual fruit must grow in community, because so many aspects of this fruit are expressed relationally. Christian community adds even more than a place to be fruitful, however. It contributes to the process by which we defeat the flesh and demonstrate spiritual fruit.

When we live in genuine *koinōnia* with one another, we share our troubles and weaknesses (Gal. 6:2), our sufferings and sicknesses (1 Cor. 12:26; James 5:14). We ought to share life so deeply that we know when others are struggling with the flesh, and they know when we are. In these vulnerable situations, we can help one another, gently and humbly, leave sin behind and return to *koinōnia* with the Spirit (Gal. 6:1–2). God binds us together in fellowship so that we might help one another become more like Christ, in heart and in deed.

Sometimes we don't mind sharing "little" sins with one another, as if there were such a thing. We can confess the sin of workaholism, for example, with an almost boastful spirit because it is so valued in our world. We can admit to a bit of envy without too much embarrassment. But those sins that ravage our souls, those sins that lock us in the dungeon of shame—these we make every effort to hide from others. In so doing, we cut ourselves off from the very community God has given to help us get free from those sins. How can my brothers and sisters help me get back on the right path if they don't know when I am overcome by some habit of sinning?

The New Testament letter of James counsels: "Confess your sins to each other and pray for each other so that you may be healed" (James 5:16). Of course, you can confess your sins directly to God without a human confessor (1 John 1:9). James is not limiting confession and forgiveness here but is offering very practical advice for how you can grow in grace. He recognizes that we cannot win the battle with sin apart from *koinōnia* with our sisters and brothers in Christ. For some reason, that is especially true when it comes to healing of deep or habitual sins. Something profoundly therapeutic happens when I let another Christian in on my failures, and when that person prays with me.

Several years ago, a woman I'll call Liz came to speak with me. I could tell from her nervousness that she was leading up to something very difficult to talk about. Finally, she gathered up enough courage to raise the issue that had devastated her heart.

"I need to tell you something I have never told anyone before," Liz began. "I don't want to talk about it now. But it's tormenting me and maybe you can help."

"Okay," I responded. "Just take your time. I'm not going anywhere."

She started to unravel a long story of a former boyfriend, a man she had expected to marry. Even though she was a strong Christian, Liz's human love for her boyfriend overwhelmed her convictions and she became sexually involved with him. For awhile she managed to squelch her guilt, but then came a surprise she could not ignore. Liz was pregnant. Mortified, she told no one about her condition, not even her boyfriend. Although she had always considered abortion to be a sin, she resolved to get an abortion as soon as possible. Liz believed that she was actually taking a human life, but the other options were too overwhelming for her even to consider.

After the abortion, Liz's shame was overpowering. She felt so bad that she couldn't even pray about what she had done. She tried to sweep it under the rug of denial. But then she'd see a newborn baby, and all of her shame would come flooding back.

Years later, Liz was happily married to a godly Christian man, not the boyfriend who once impregnated her. She was flourishing in many areas of life. But her guilt haunted her like a ghost that would never be exorcised. Finally, she worked up the courage, more out of desperation than anything else, to confess her sin to another person. She hoped I could help her get free.

After she finished her story, I asked a simple question: "Have you ever confessed this sin specifically to God?"

"No," she admitted, "I can't bring myself to say the words. It makes the whole thing seem too real."

I read a few passages of Scripture to Liz, especially the promise of 1 John 1:9: "'If we confess our sins to him, [God] is faithful and just to forgive us and to cleanse us from every wrong.' From every wrong," I repeated, "from *every* wrong."

"Let me tell you what I'd like to do," I said. "In a moment we're going to pray. I'm going to start and pray for you. I will ask the Holy Spirit to help you confess your sin. I know this is scary, but I believe God will help you. When I'm done praying, I want you to pray out loud. Take your time. Use whatever words come to you. I'll be here praying and supporting you."

When Liz agreed, we started to pray. I asked the Lord to help her confess and then waited. She began slowly, awkwardly, trying to find words for that which she had never before said. Finally, with many tears, she began to pour out her heart to God. She admitted what she had done. She held nothing back from her Savior.

When Liz finished praying, I asked God to confirm his forgiveness to her. Then I took up my Bible once again and read, "'If we confess our sins to him, [God] is faithful and just to forgive us and to cleanse us from every wrong.' From every wrong. Cleansed from *every* wrong. Liz, God has forgiven you for everything. He has cleansed you completely. You are forgiven!"

I'll never forget the look on Liz's face. Exhausted, emotionally spent, she nevertheless glowed with God's peace. Her tears of anguish became tears of joy as she basked in her forgiveness. That moment in my office sparked a series of stunning transformations in Liz's life. Her new experience of grace gave her internal peace and the power to live for God in ways she never would have anticipated. Her shame had blocked the flow of the Spirit in her life. When it was removed, Liz's life abounded with the fruit of the Spirit.

I almost didn't include this story here because it seems to place too much importance on pastors, as if we are the only ones who can help people receive divine healing for their sins. Because pastors sometimes feel "safe" to people, we can serve as effective confessors. But, ideally, our *koinōnia* as brothers and sisters in Christ should also be a "priesthood of all believers," a community in which we serve as confessors to one another, without regard to official position in church (James 5:16; 1 Peter 2:9).

If we are ever to reach this level of mutual intimacy, it will only happen through committed, long-term, close relationships among Christian brothers and sisters. I have witnessed this kind of openness rarely in my Christian life. When it occurs, it happens in small groups, in discipleship relationships, in spiritual direction, or in abiding prayer partnerships.

Moreover, we will only feel the freedom to share our deepest struggles with others if our Christian community fosters this kind of vulnerability. Only when our fellow believers humbly acknowledge their own sin and recognize that they are saved by grace alone will we risk telling them the secrets of our lives. It's hard for churches to preserve the right balance between a solid commitment to biblical holiness and, at the same time, a Christ-like love for unholy sinners. Yet it is precisely this balance for which we must strive if we are to form communities in which people—ourselves included—can truly find freedom from sin.

Intimate fellowship with God and with people enables us to gain victory over the flesh and to manifest the fruit of the Spirit in our lives. These successes lead, in turn, to still deeper *koinōnia* with God and our Christian family. The bondage of sin and shame is broken through the power of God as we are transformed inside and out.

PRACTICAL QUESTIONS AND ANSWERS

1. "I haven't been a Christian for very long, but I am eager to get on the right track for personal transformation. What should I do?"

Simply do what the Scripture says: "Keep on walking in the Holy Spirit!" (Gal. 5:16). Don't put all of your effort into avoiding sin and doing good deeds, even though you should avoid sin and do good deeds. Rather, invest yourself in developing deeper koinōnia *with the Spirit of God.*

Let me suggest three crucial steps in this process. First, embrace the truth of who you are in Christ. You are a beloved child of God. You are a saint in whom the Holy Spirit dwells. Even when you sin, you are still one who has been made right with God through Christ.

Second, set your mind on the things of the Spirit (Rom. 8:5). The more you focus on the things of God, the more you will be transformed (Rom. 12:1–2). Are you filling your mind with God's truth on a regular basis through studying the Bible? Are you meditating on God's Word?

Third, share in genuine fellowship with the community of the Spirit. Remember that life in the Spirit is not a solitary endeavor, even though special times of solitude are important. If you are not committed to a church, make this a top priority. If you are part of a church but not in a place for intimate fellowship with other Christians, find a prayer group, a small Bible study, or some other context where you can share your victories and your struggles with other Christians.

2. "I'm one of those people who is stuck in sin. I keep on doing that which I hate. I have confessed hundreds of times. I have made resolutions. I have felt what seemed like genuine sorrow. But I'm still stuck. What should I do?"

Let me begin by reminding you of the good news. In the preface to his commentary on Romans, Martin Luther wrote:

The Holy Spirit assures us that *we are God's children no matter how furiously sin may rage within us*, so long as we follow the Spirit and struggle against sin in order to kill it.[3]

The fact that you struggle against your sin proves that you are a child of God, even if your efforts have been unsuccessful so far. Luther's encouragement here is so important because when we are stuck in sin, we tend to focus on our sin and our feelings of shame. When we get obsessed with the sin in our life, even to avoid it, ironically, we end up sinning even more.

Because you are stuck in sin, I'd expect that one or more of the following is true about you: 1. You have focused on your failure rather than on Christ; 2. Your personal time with God is irregular; 3. You have not shared your struggle with another Christian who can be praying for you and holding you accountable. If any of these are true about you, you know what to do. Focus on Christ! Spend quality time with your heavenly Father! Confess your sin to a brother or a sister so you can be healed! (James 5:16).

11
Intimate Fellowship and Love

My daughter, Kara, loves a love story. Even though she is only six years old, she is romantic to the depths of her young soul. When she saw the recent movie version of Tarzan, for example, Kara was intrigued by the state-of-the-art animation, the Oscar-winning music, and the clever story line. But most of all she "LOVED" the closing scene when Tarzan and Jane finally kiss. Kara is a hopeless romantic.

That's how my son, Nathan, sees her. He is more into action than "silly" romance. The fact that Kara can reduce an action film like *Star Wars* to a love story insults Nathan's eight-year-old machismo. When Kara gushes about the kissing scenes of a film, Nathan rolls his eyes and lets out annoyed sighs. But when no one is looking, even Nathan can enjoy a good love story, no matter how much he denies it.

The Christian Love Story

Christianity is a love story. It's not the sappy, squishy kind of love story. No Harlequin romance here. But it is, nonetheless, a love story—one that is deeper, truer, and more compelling than any other.

The story begins with a God who loved us even before he created us to live with him in an intimate relationship of holy love (Eph. 1:3–4). When we spurned God's love, he did not reject us (Lam. 3:31). Even though we chased after other lovers, God pursued us with an unfailing love (Hos. 3:1–5; 11:8). Ultimately, God's love moved him to send his very own Son to give up his life as a revelation of God's irrepressible love for us (John 3:16; Rom. 5:8). Jesus, the Son of God, not only revealed God's love but also embodied and delivered that love to us through his sacrifice on the cross (Rom. 5:8; 1 John 4:9).

The Christian love story continues as we respond to God's love. Our initial response is to accept that love through faith in Christ. When we do this, we are restored into loving fellowship with God, and we also experience the pouring out of God's love in our hearts (Rom. 5:5).

As we experience the transforming love of God, we become people who love with new freedom. First John 4:19 puts it succinctly: "We love because he first loved us" (NIV). Whom do we love? First, we love God with all of our heart, soul, mind, and strength (Mark 12:30). Second, we love our neighbor and even our enemy (Mark 12:31; Luke 6:35). John puts the matter more bluntly in his first letter:

> If someone says, "I love God," but hates a Christian brother or sister, that person is a liar; for if we don't love people we can see, how can we love God, whom we have not seen? And God himself has commanded that we must love not only him but our Christian brothers and sisters, too.
>
> 1 John 4:20–21

Positively, if we love one another, John promises, "God lives in us, and his love has been brought to full expression through us" (1 John 4:12). Our loving *koinōnia* with other Christians leads to the completion of God's love in us.

The Christian story, therefore, is a dramatic love story: love given, love rejected, love overcoming, love received, love poured out, love transforming, love returned, love given away.

What is Love?

We use the word *love* in such varied ways that its meaning can get lost in a haze of ambiguity. We love our children, our parents, and our new pair of shoes. We love our country, our freedom, and hot dogs. Love explains why a woman will sit patiently by her invalid husband's bedside for years, and it is brandished by a teenager who wants to have sex with his girlfriend. Love motivates heroes to risk their lives, and it sells millions of pop music CDs. Is it any wonder that we might ask, What is love? People have been puzzling over this question for centuries. In fact, as I am writing this chapter while sitting in Einstein's Bagels, a song blares over the radio with these telling words: "What is love, anyway?"[1]

The Bible answers this question directly: "This is real love. It is not that we loved God, but that he loved us and sent his Son as a sacrifice to take away our sins" (1 John 4:10). God reveals the true nature of love by the gift of his Son, who came to die for us. *Love is an act of self-giving for the sake of another. Love is the active commitment of yourself to what is best for someone else, even if that commitment requires the sacrifice of your very life.* True love is not anything we want it to be. It is defined by God, by his revelation in Christ (1 John 3:16). According to God, love is ultimate self-giving.

It's possible and even laudable to love your children and parents that way, but not your shoes. Many people have genuinely loved their country and freedom, but not hot dogs. True love explains why a woman sits faithfully by her dying husband's bedside, but it has nothing to do with the self-centered desires of teenage eroticism. Real love can motivate heroes to risk their lives, but it is absent from most popular music.

In biblical perspective, love is more an activity than a feeling. Although certain feelings will often join themselves to love, these feelings are not the essence of biblical love. When Jesus tells us to love our neighbors, he doesn't expect us to sit back and feel fondly about them. He wants us to give ourselves actively in service to them.

Love: The Ultimate Priority for the Christian

Given the love story dimension of Christianity, it comes as no surprise that love is the pinnacle of life. According to Scripture, love is the ultimate priority, the supreme value, the most prized activity of the Christian life.

According to Jesus, the Old Testament call to love God is "the first and greatest commandment" (Matt. 22:38). Love for people also takes priority in Jesus' teaching and ministry. After exemplifying the self-giving nature of love by washing the feet of his disciples, Jesus explains that love should be the definitive characteristic of their fellowship: "So now I am giving you a new commandment: Love each other. Just as I have loved you, you should love each other. Your love for one another will prove to the world that you are my disciples" (John 13:34–35).

The supremacy of love for the Christian is a thread woven throughout the whole New Testament (see Rom. 13:8–10;

1 Peter 4:8; 1 John 4:7–12). When summing up how we ought to live as Christians, Paul writes:

> Since God chose you to be the holy people *whom he loves,* you must clothe yourselves with tenderhearted mercy, kindness, humility, gentleness, and patience. . . . *And the most important piece of clothing you must wear is love. Love is what binds us all together in perfect harmony.*
>
> Colossians 3:12–14, italics added

How Are We to Love?

We find an answer to this question in Ephesians 5: "Therefore, *be imitators of God,* as his beloved children, and *keep on living in love, as Christ also loved us* and gave himself for us as a sacrifice and fragrant offering to God" (Eph. 5:1–2 MDR, italics added). We love by imitating God through living in love.

Loving like God is easier said than done, of course. Even when we have been redeemed and reconciled to God, the remnants of our sinful nature keep popping up, causing us to put self-interest above the interest of others. For this reason we must "*keep on* living in love." We do this by remembering Christ's death for us each day, by regularly spending time with our heavenly Father, by continually enjoying our *koinōnia* with the Spirit of God and with God's people.

You may recall that in our earlier investigation of the fruit of the Spirit, love was mentioned as the first quality of that fruit (Gal. 5:22). The Spirit helps us to love, teaching us how to love the people around us (1 Thess. 4:9–10). The Spirit also softens our hearts and energizes our bodies for service.

Loving through Spiritual Gifts

We see the close connection between love and the Spirit especially in 1 Corinthians 12–14. Here, in the center of his explanation of how the Spirit empowers us for ministry, Paul pens the so-called "Love Chapter": "If I speak in the tongues of men and of angels, but have not love, I am only a resounding gong or a clanging cymbal. . . . Love is patient, love is kind" (1 Cor. 13:1, 4 NIV). Paul's poetic description of love often adorns weddings, but it wasn't written for this purpose. Rather, Paul penned his praise of love as a corrective for the Corinthians. These immature believers were valuing their own spiritual experiences more than anything, including their Christian siblings. If they experienced some kind of miracle, they became puffed up with pride and even denigrated those whose spiritual résumés were less impressive. Paul wanted to encourage the Corinthians to expect miracles by the Spirit, but he also wanted to reshape their understanding of the purpose of these wonders. Supernatural experiences are not badges of spiritual honor but gifts from God and tools for ministry. They are endowments of the Holy Spirit, bestowed on Christians, for the purpose of ministering to others and building up the church.

After waxing poetic about love in 1 Corinthians 13, Paul urges his readers to put their eagerness for miracles on this foundation: "Pursue love; eagerly desire spiritual gifts" (1 Cor. 14:1 MDR). Spiritual gifts are given not primarily for the benefit of the one who ministers but for the sake of those who receive the ministry, the ultimate recipients of the gifts.

Paul mentions many different kinds of spiritual gifts, including a word of wisdom, a word of knowledge, faith, workings of powers, prophesying, discernment of spirits, kinds of tongues, and interpretation of tongues (1 Cor. 12:8–10; see also 1 Cor. 12:28–31; Rom. 12:6–11). All of these gifts, and others besides, are given according to the will of the Spirit to build up the church (1 Cor. 12:4–11). If we want to excel in the exercise of spiritual gifts, we should pursue love above everything else.

Several years ago, while I was pastoring at Hollywood Presbyterian Church, I had an experience that epitomized the inseparable connection between love and spiritual gifts. One day, a woman named Maria came to the church seeking financial assistance. She was a single mother who was the sole support for her family. Maria had been struggling with a mysterious physical condition that covered her legs with debilitating, painful, oozing sores. She was so poor that she couldn't get appropriate medical assistance. A doctor in a clinic told Maria that an operation might help her, but she couldn't afford it. Her physical condition deteriorated so much that she lost her job. She came to the church to get financial help for her family and perhaps some money for pain medication. The church was able to provide her with some financial assistance, but her problems seemed overwhelming, far beyond what we could handle.

Before Maria left, I asked if I could pray for her. My wife, Linda, and our friend Nancy were nearby, so the three of us sat with Maria, laid hands on her, and began to pray. As we interceded for Maria, we all felt powerful love for her, great compassion for her suffering. We poured out our hearts to God, seeking his help for this woman. We prayed for her finances, for her family, and especially for her legs to be healed. How could we love her without crying out to God for healing? Or, to use Paul's language, how could we pursue love for Maria without eagerly desiring a spiritual gift of healing for her?

After we finished praying, Maria said she felt God's presence. She knew that God loved her in a way she had never known before. Linda, Nancy, and I were glad but a bit disappointed that God didn't do something to heal Maria's legs. That was the last we ever saw of Maria.

Three months later, I received a phone call at church. "This is Maria," an unfamiliar voice said, "I am calling to thank you."

"Maria, Maria," I repeated, trying to place the voice. "I am so sorry, but I don't remember who you are."

"Oh," she said, "I'm the one with those terrible leg sores. Don't you remember that you and your friends prayed for me?"

"Of course I do. I'm sorry I forgot your name."

"I'm back at work now," Maria continued, "and I wanted to thank you."

"You are certainly welcome," I said, "but we didn't do much at all. We gave you some money for your medicine, but that's about it. I wish we could have done more."

"Oh, you did do more! Don't you remember? You prayed for me to be healed. Remember? I'm calling to thank you because your prayer worked. Very soon after I left your church, my legs began to get better. They kept on getting better. My doctor couldn't believe it. In a few days, I could return to work. Now I'm just fine. God healed my legs. I want to thank you for praying for me."

To this day, I marvel at that whole experience. What a joy to be used by God in such a special way! That time of prayer for Maria serves as a paradigm for my ongoing ministry in the Spirit. My job as a Christian is to love people. If they are suffering, that love motivates me to pray. If they are sick, I seek a gift of healing for them. If they need guidance, I ask for a gift of wisdom. If they don't know Christ, I seek a gift of evangelism. The results of my seeking are usually not as dramatic as in the case of Maria, but that's not my responsibility. You and I can't guarantee what the Spirit will do when we step out to minister, but if we love, if we make ourselves available, and if we pray, God's work will be done. People will be healed, saved, and loved. The body of Christ will be built up. And you and I will have the joy of being used by God in his marvelous work of love.

Love in and out of Bounds

Jesus said that our love for one another would prove to the world that we are his disciples (John 13:34–35). The command for Christians to love other Christians reverberates throughout the New Testament (for example, John 15:12; Rom. 12:10; 1 Peter 1:22; 1 John 4:7). Love should be the defining characteristic of our life within the Christian family (1 Peter 2:17).

But Jesus also commands us to love beyond the bounds deemed acceptable by society. We should love even our enemies (Matt. 5:43–45). In this manner, we imitate the love of God, a love that is not limited to those who love him back.

Jesus often loved "out of bounds." He spent time with tax collectors and sinners, those who were despised by the Jewish religious elite (Mark 2:15–16). Moved with pity, Jesus touched a leper to heal him, even though this physical contact rendered Jesus himself ritually unclean (Mark 1:40–42). He allowed a woman of ill repute to wash and kiss his feet, while anointing them with expensive perfume (Luke 7:36–38). He even healed the servant of a Roman centurion, an officer whose presence in Israel represented the despised rule of Rome (Matt. 8:5–13).

All of us have opportunities to love "out of bounds." We all have people who are the last folks we'd choose to love. Yet, we are still called to love them with a Christ-like love.

My mother loves in a way that imitates Jesus' love, and I have experienced this love thousands of times. I have seen it given to many others, especially to a young man named Rick.

Rick came to live with my parents when my father was dying of cancer. He was a friend of my sister, a loving man who cheered up my parents with his humor, his kindness, and his excellent cooking. Rick also happened to be gay. He was not a Christian, so he didn't feel that he was doing anything wrong through his sexual activities.

My mother made it clear to Rick that she believed homosexual behavior to be wrong and asked him to respect her values in her home. During the months of Rick's stay, they had many discussions about the most important things in life, not only sexuality. They talked about family, love, God, and dozens of other subjects. Over time, Rick began to feel like a member of our family as he shared our joys and sorrows, our holiday celebrations, and our long vigils at my dad's bedside.

There was never a shred of doubt in Rick's mind about my mother's views on his sexual behavior. He knew that she did not approve. Nor did he doubt her love for him, a love that was demonstrated in many ways. The relationship of love between Rick and my family was mutual, especially as he walked with us through an extremely difficult season in our life together.

Some time after my father died, Rick discovered that he was HIV positive. In those days, medical treatment was not very advanced, and he quickly developed full-blown AIDS. During that painful time, Rick continued to be loved by my family. He eventually moved home to Canada to spend his last few months with his own family.

My mother visited Rick shortly before he died. Once again, they talked about God and about what it means to be a Christian. Through much suffering, Rick had come to realize his need for God and God's forgiveness. He finally put his trust in Jesus. Rick's own imminent death, a great loss for those of us who loved him, would be his eternal gain. He is with the Lord today, in part because my mother was willing to love "out of bounds," just as Jesus did.

Transformed by Love to Love Others

There are times, however, when we need intensive care from the Spirit to become loving people. Some of us have experienced deep emotional wounds that damage our ability to give and to receive love. Children who have been neglected or abused, victims of violent crime, or those who have been cruelly rejected by a parent or a spouse, all of these can find it very difficult to open their hearts to love. Often these folks experience significant healing at the moment of their conversion. Usually this is just the start of an ongoing process of transformation through the Holy Spirit.

Paul reveals that "the love of God has been poured into our hearts through the Holy Spirit that was given to us" (Rom. 5:5 MDR). The Holy Spirit, Paul says, drenches us with the love of God. This isn't a one-time experience. The perfect verb in the verse could be literally translated: "the love of God *has been poured with continuing effect* into our hearts." What began when the Spirit was first given to us continues as we experience deeper *koinōnia* with the Spirit. As we are showered with God's love, we are healed, transformed, and empowered to love in ways we could never have loved before.

I have known that God loves me for as long as I can remember. I grew up in a loving family with parents and grandparents who often spoke of God's love. I accepted Christ when I was six years old and have lived since then with certainty about God's love for me. But my experience of God's love has been more intellectual than affective. I have known about God's love more than I have known his love in a personal way. At times, however, the Holy Spirit has poured divine love into my heart, forever changing me.

During my father's slow death from cancer, my life was in turmoil, stirred up by my dad's sickness and by a new marriage, a new ministry, and the dark cloud of my unfinished dissertation. One Sunday evening my wife and I visited a church that was known to have a lively worship service. At the close of the service, the congregation celebrated communion. The elements and meaning were familiar, but the forms quite unfamiliar. Rather than coming forward to receive the bread and wine, or passing it along rows, we gathered in small groups to serve one another. I didn't like this arrangement because I am, by nature, a shy person. We were instructed to serve one another and then to pray quietly while waiting on the Spirit. If we felt led to ask for prayer or to pray for someone else, we should follow the Spirit's lead.

After receiving the elements, I prayed silently with my eyes tightly closed. I tried to forget the people around me. All of a sudden, I began to feel the presence of God in a way I had only known once or twice before. It was as if the Holy Spirit were bathing me in the warm, cleansing love of God. I didn't know exactly what was happening to me, but I was simply delighting in the presence of God. Tears came to my eyes as God's love kept pouring into me. After two or three minutes, I opened my eyes, surprised to find my little group gathered about me and praying silently. Because they had not touched me or said anything, I hadn't known what they were doing. When I asked why they were praying for me, one said, "We sensed that the Spirit wanted to minister to you, so we prayed for whatever he wanted to do." Under normal circumstances, I would have felt exceedingly embarrassed to receive such attention, but with the love of God still filling my heart, I simply felt grateful for the sensitive care of these unfamiliar brothers and sisters.

On the way home from that service, I tried to sort out what the Spirit was doing. I knew that I had received a wonderful infilling of God's love, but I wasn't exactly sure why. I figured that the Lord was probably encouraging me in a time when my life was so stressful. In retrospect, I think that's partly true. But God was up to something more.

I didn't tell many people what happened to me in that communion service. In the weeks that followed, however, I kept hearing a comment from a wide variety of sources. A couple of my colleagues at church said, "Mark, there is something different about you. You seem more peaceful, more compassionate and caring for others." Family members made similar observations. Though I didn't seem that different to myself, my behavior had truly changed. As the Spirit poured the love of God into my heart, I was healed and transformed to love in fresh ways.

I know many other people who have had dramatic encounters with the love of God poured out through the Spirit. Most of the time, however, divine love comes in smaller servings, and they encourage us in our Christian walk, draw us into deeper *koinōnia* with God, and transform us to love others more freely.

Love and *Koinōnia*

Often God's love comes to us through those same "others." The Spirit can pour love into our hearts directly, of course, but he frequently uses others as conduits for the flow. When our Christian siblings care for us, pray for us, encourage us, and forgive us, we sense not just human love but divine love given through human channels.

It's easy to see why love is essential to Christian *koinōnia*. We enter into intimate fellowship with God because of his love for us in Christ. That same love binds us together with other believers so that our mutual love might demonstrate our discipleship to the world. Love among Christians is a sign of intimate fellowship and a means by which that fellowship grows deeper and deeper.

But we often don't form genuine, open relationships with one another because of fear. We are afraid that if others really knew us, they'd reject us. If you could actually see into my heart, if you knew my failures and my doubts, would you really want to read this book? I'm not sure. Maybe you wouldn't even want to be my friend. You'd probably feel a similar fear about revealing yourself to me.

Sometimes we're afraid to reveal not only the unseemly parts of ourselves but also the most precious, tender, and wonderful parts. If I share my deepest hopes with you, will you embrace them or minimize them? If I admit to loving Hardy Boys mystery books and Superman movies, will you think I'm silly? If you find out that I tear up during Kodak commercials, just like my mother whom I always scorned for being so emotional, will you laugh at me like I laughed at her?

What will set us free to be ourselves with one another and even with God? Only God's perfect love for us. Because we have his love, we have no fear of standing before God's throne in the final judgment. "There is no fear in love," John writes, "but perfect love casts out fear" (1 John 4:18 MDR). John looks ahead to the most vulnerable moment of all, to what should also be the scariest time of life, when we stand alone before the judgment seat of God. Nothing about us will be hidden; everything will be revealed. Yet we can have confidence that God's love for us will be rock solid in that moment. So, as we look ahead to judgment, and as we live in God right now, his perfect love takes away our fear. Just think of it for a moment. When you stand before God, when every part of you is exposed to the light of his judgment, you will be declared "Not Guilty" because of what God's love for you has done in Christ. What a life-changing vision! Can you begin to taste the freedom of God's love?

The perfect love of God takes away our fear of intimacy with him. When we realize that we are eternally loved and forgiven, we discover new freedom to approach God no matter how we have failed. We don't have to hold anything back. We don't have to hide or pretend or exaggerate or put on a pious face for God. We can be truly who we are and still be 100 percent assured of God's loving acceptance.

The experience of God's perfect love carries over into the rest of life. "As we live in God," John observes, "our love grows more perfect" (1 John 4:17). The love of God transforms us so that we begin to love as he loves. Moreover, we are set free from the fear that keeps us from sharing our true selves with one another. Our greater openness will lead to deeper *koinōnia*, which will in turn provide more opportunities for us to love. Thus, love *flows from* and *contributes to* our intimate fellowship with God and with one another.

Fathoming the Unfathomable Love of God

God has demonstrated his love for us through the sacrifice of his Son. God has poured his love into our hearts through the Holy Spirit. You would think, therefore, that it wouldn't be too hard for us to internalize God's love. Unfortunately, this is not usually the case. Surely, we can say that God loves us, and we can believe what we say, at least partly. But, time and again, we who know about God's love act as if we aren't quite sure about it. We run away from God when we sin or question his goodness when we suffer. We do this because, on the one hand, our limited minds cannot fully comprehend God's love. It exceeds our intellectual abilities. The brightest people in all of human history could spend eternity peering into God's love and still only begin to plumb its depths. On the other hand, our hearts paradoxically resist accepting the most excellent and comforting news there is. The love of God feels just too good to be true.

To help us understand and experience God's love, Jesus tells the "Parable of the Prodigal Son" (Luke 15:11–32). A father has two sons; the elder is the classic "good boy" while the younger cares only about his selfish pleasures. This son insults his father by asking for his inheritance even before his father has died. In effect, the son says, "I'm going to treat you as if you were dead, Dad. So fork over the dough right now." Surprisingly, the father endures this insult and gives his son his share of the inheritance. The son heads off to the ancient version of Las Vegas to enjoy his wealth, where he quickly squanders it on loose living. No doubt about it, he is the wasteful one, the *prodigal* son.

In time, a famine devastates the land where this son is living, and he has no money left to provide for his needs. He resorts to feeding pigs, the lowliest job a Jewish boy could imagine. As he doles out the pig slop, he finds himself wishing he could eat it himself. At this point, the boy comes to his senses. He realizes that his father's servants eat better than he does. He resolves to return to his father, to confess his unworthiness, and to beg to become one of the servants. With this plan in mind, he abandons the pigs and heads for home.

When the son is just barely visible on the horizon, his father sees him. "Filled with love and compassion, he ran to his son, embraced him, and kissed him" (Luke 15:20). The perplexed son can't even get out his confession speech before his father has showered him with love and evidence of his acceptance back into the family. To top things off, the father throws a giant party to celebrate his son's return. Indeed, the

183

father is really the "prodigal" one, the one who loves profusely, extravagantly, beyond the bounds of appropriateness.[2]

That's how God loves us, Jesus says, with this kind of impossible love—with a love that bears insults, gives generously, yearns for reconciliation, rushes to embrace us when we repent, celebrates our arrival home, and embraces us as beloved members of the heavenly family. God's love for you is like that of a "prodigal" parent, one who lavishes love beyond all reasonable measure. God loves you more ferociously and tenderly than you love anyone or anything. And no matter what you do, no matter how poorly you return his love, no matter how you might wander away from God, his love will never let you go.

> Can anything ever separate us from Christ's love? Does it mean he no longer loves us if we have trouble or calamity, or are persecuted, or are hungry or cold or in danger or threatened with death? . . . No, despite all these things, overwhelming victory is ours through Christ, who loved us. And I am convinced that nothing can ever separate us from his love. Death can't, and life can't. The angels can't, and the demons can't. Our fears for today, our worries about tomorrow, and even the powers of hell can't keep God's love away. Whether we are high above the sky or in the deepest ocean, nothing in all creation will ever be able to separate us from the love of God that is revealed in Christ Jesus our Lord.
>
> Rom. 8:35, 37–39

PRACTICAL QUESTIONS AND ANSWERS

1. "All of this stuff about God's love sounds great, but I'm just not sure that he really loves me. How can I be sure?"

Assurance of God's love comes as you meditate on the cross, the ultimate sign of God's love for you. Remember that "God showed his great love for us by sending Christ to die for us while we were still sinners" (Rom. 5:8 NLT). Take time alone with God to reflect on the fact and meaning of Christ's sacrifice for you.

Assurance also comes as the love of God in Christ is celebrated in Christian community. Preaching, prayers, hymns, and songs proclaim God's love and help our hearts to absorb that which our intellects affirm. Most of all, the Lord's Supper allows us to remember and to experience afresh the love of Christ. If you are not regularly worshipping with a Christian community, find a church where you can celebrate the love of Christ with others.

It might be that something is blocking your internalization of God's love for you. Habitual sin can harden your heart to the Lord. Woundedness from the past can keep you from opening up to God. If God's love continues to feel distant, I encourage you to share your struggle with a mature Christian who can listen sensitively and pray faithfully.

There are times when, for his own reasons, God appears to withdraw the immediacy of his presence from us. Surely he is still with us and the Spirit remains within us, but it feels to us as if God has hidden himself. In these times we cry out with the psalmist: "O LORD, why do you stand so far away? Why do you hide when I need you the most?" (Ps. 10:1). In these times of wandering in the desert, we especially need the community of brothers and sisters in Christ to uphold and to encourage us. In time, God will refresh us in his love (Zeph. 3:17).

2. **"We are supposed to love our enemies. Jesus loved even infamous sinners, such as tax collectors and prostitutes. But I am afraid that loving sinners will give them the idea that I approve of their behavior. I don't want to do this, so I am reluctant to love those who are living in obvious sin. What should I do?"**

I have heard this sort of question many times related to a variety of situations. It has come from parents, for example, whose children are living in ways that dishonor God. An adult son moves in with his girlfriend and expects his family to treat them as a married couple. Parents wonder how they can love their son and his girlfriend without endorsing their cohabitation. Or a grown daughter announces that she is planning to "marry" her lesbian girlfriend and invites her parents to the service. They wonder what love means in a situation like this.

First, remember that loving people does not mean failing to tell the truth to them. Our culture falsely equates love with affirmation and approval. If you love someone, we are told, you must approve of that person's behavior. Or if you don't approve, you shouldn't say anything because "it wouldn't be loving." Scripture views love and truth from a completely different viewpoint. Throughout the Bible God tells us the truth, often very painful truth about our sin, precisely because he does love us. Similarly, we are to "speak the truth in love" (Eph. 4:15 MDR). If a person you love is doing something sinful, love itself requires honest, humble communication.

I tell parents that they should humbly but firmly tell their children what they think about their sexual relationships without withdrawing love. Moreover, if they have been honest about their convictions, parents do not have to back away from active relationships with their children. This sort of withdrawal confuses love and approval in the other direction, something many Christians do. Like Jesus, we must love people even when we don't approve of their behavior. To illustrate this point, I often tell the story of my mother's love for Rick.

God calls you to love the people in your life as he has loved you in Christ. Sometimes your love will lead you to say hard things. Sometimes your love will lead you to walk a second mile or give up the shirt on your back (Matt. 5:40–41). Sometimes your love will lead you into situations that are awkward, where your behavior could be misconstrued as approving sin. Don't worry. That's what Jesus did. No matter where you find yourself, keep on loving.

12

Intimate Fellowship and Peace

In our nerve-racking world, plenty of people offer peace—for a price. Automobile manufacturers hawk peace in the form of perfectly engineered cars. Insurance companies promise serenity to those who purchase comprehensive insurance policies. Pharmaceutical companies market peace through Prozac. The New Age movement tempts us with Millennium Peace Crystals. Pricey workshops promise to restore peace to marriages once we discover who we are as "Mars" and "Venus." Travel agents trump these offers with the lure of getting away from it all. Peace awaits us on a secluded beach on some faraway island, where we can let the stresses of life evaporate in the hot sun, at least until our travelers checks or our vacation days run out.

We are rightly skeptical when faced with offers of peace, whether they come from corporations or therapeutic gurus. How then ought we respond to Jesus, who once said, "I'm leaving you with a gift—peace of mind and heart. And the peace I give isn't like the peace the world gives. So don't be troubled or afraid" (John 14:27)? Why should we believe that Jesus can actually deliver the unique peace he promises?

The Peace of Jesus

To understand why Jesus can fulfill his promise of peace, we must first know more about the peace he offers and why it is needed. The peace of Jesus is far more than merely a lack of conflict. He offers what is captured in the Hebrew word for peace, *shalom*. We sometimes think of peace as the absence of war, but *shalom* includes notions of wholeness and prosperity (Ps. 37:11; Isa. 54:1–17). When peace fills the land, justice and righteousness abound (Isa. 32:15–17; Ps. 85:10).

God created the earth to be a place of peace. We see this clearly in the creation account of Genesis. In the Garden of Eden, human beings enjoy flawless relationships with their creator, with each other, and even with the earth (Gen. 2:15, 25). Wholeness and righteousness abound in the peaceful Garden under God's loving reign.

Unfortunately, the human story doesn't end with Genesis 2. In Genesis 3, the man and the woman rebel against God and his rule over their lives. All of a sudden the peace God intended for creation is shattered by human sin. Adam and Eve hide from each other, from themselves, and even from God, revealing the loss of peace in their hearts and their key relationships (Gen. 3:7–8). Moreover, although God intended humans to live forever in his peace, now they will die, both physically and spiritually (Gen. 3:19). As the ultimate proof of sin's devastation, God banishes Adam and Eve from the peaceful Garden.

But God did not abandon humankind forever. In the Old Testament, he promises to mend that which had been lost in the Garden by reestablishing his reign and the peace that flows from it. Someday he will make a "covenant of peace" with his people (Ezek. 37:26). At that time, the people will shout joyfully: "How beautiful on the mountains are the feet of those who bring good news of peace and salvation, the news that the God of Israel reigns!" (Isa. 52:7). When God saves, he will restore his kingdom so that those who live under his rule will experience the fullness of peace.

That restoration begins inauspiciously in a stable outside of a small village in Judea. Yet when Jesus is born, a vast heavenly choir sings before an enthralled congregation of sheep and shepherds: "Glory to God in the highest heaven, and peace on earth to all whom God favors" (Luke 2:14). Peace on earth, finally! This sounds just great, doesn't it? It also sounds like something promised on a tacky poster in a college dorm, or like the failed slogan of a former world leader.

Neville Chamberlain was prime minister of Great Britain in 1938, a time of crisis in Europe. In March of that year, Adolf Hitler led Germany to devour Austria. Then, turning his eyes toward Czechoslovakia, Hitler drew up a plan to take over that nation as well. As war between Germany and Czechoslovakia seemed imminent, the Czechs looked to their allies, France and Britain, for help. But the French and the British were eager to avoid a war with Hitler's dominant military machine. In September 1938, Prime Minister Chamberlain, in partnership with French leaders, began negotiations with Hitler. Things appeared hopeless, however, because the Führer insisted on Germany's right to a substantial portion of Czechoslovakia. Yet Chamberlain was so eager to avoid war that he caved in to Hitler's demands in return for his promise to resolve all future differences through consultation rather than military action. In October 1938, Chamberlain announced to jubilant crowds throughout Britain that he had achieved "peace with honour. I believe it is peace in our time." Of course, we know the rest of the story. Within months, Hitler had taken over the rest of Czechoslovakia and had invaded Poland as well. "Peace in our time" was no peace at all because it failed to remedy the root cause of the strife: Hitler's plan to dominate Europe.

The peace on earth celebrated by the angelic choir outside of Bethlehem won't add up to a hill of beans unless it resolves the root cause of human brokenness. The one who brings peace must be able to remove the stain of human sin, that which disrupted peace in the first place. This is exactly why Jesus came into the world (1 Tim. 1:15). Peace didn't come, however, merely because of his birth. World-transforming peace isn't a by-product of Christmas cheer. Jesus' birth was only a prerequisite to his final peacemaking effort, something we celebrate during Holy Week, not Christmas. As the Word of God made fully human, Jesus represented us on the cross. His death and resurrection dealt a fatal blow to sin, the root cause of human brokenness. Because Jesus was crucified and was raised from the dead, we can have peace in all of its fullness: "For God in all his fullness was pleased to live in Christ, and by him God reconciled everything to himself. He made peace with everything in heaven and on earth by means of his blood on the cross" (Col. 1:19–20). For this reason, Paul says simply of Christ: "He himself is our peace" (Eph. 2:14 NIV).

What kind of peace can we expect to experience through believing in Jesus? To begin with, when we trust in him, we have peace with God (Rom. 5:1). Although we were once God's enemies because of sin, now because of Christ we are God's friends (Rom. 5:10–11). The strife between us and the Lord has been overcome by his grace. We can enjoy koinō-nia with God as citizens of his kingdom. Peace with God also encompasses everything God had intended for creation, including peace within ourselves and peace with others.

Inner Peace

Jesus promises to give his followers supernatural peace, and he provides this peace through the mediation of the Holy Spirit. It isn't like the peace offered by the world, which depends on outward circumstances or inward rationalizations. Indeed, God's peace often comes when events or reasons would provide just cause for worry. It "is far more wonderful than the human mind can understand" (Phil. 4:7).

If you've never experienced the peace of Christ, these claims can sound unrealistic. But millions of Christians have known inexplicable peace in situations that would seem to instill distress. The great hymn writer, Charles Wesley, who wrote such beloved songs as "Hark! The Herald Angels Sing," lived a full life of service to Christ. Early in his seventy-ninth year, however, his health began to falter. As sickness dominated his body, Wesley knew that he would soon die. His doctor, who regularly visited his bedside during the last days, described Wesley's attitude in the face of death:

> He possessed that state of mind which he had been always pleased to see in others—unaffected humility, and holy resignation to the will of God. He had no transports of joy, but solid hope and unshaken confidence in Christ, which kept his mind in perfect peace.[1]

Another well-known hymn writer celebrated God's perfect peace in song. Frances Havergal, who penned many hymns, including "Take My Life, and Let It Be," lived a short and painful life. When she was eleven, her mother died. Shortly thereafter, her father remarried. Frances's stepmother came between her and her father, causing deep hurt to the girl. As a young adult, Frances became so ill that she struggled even to get out of bed. Yet she continued to live actively,

191

writing dozens of hymns. During one of her periods of illness, she composed these words:

> Like a river glorious,
> Is God's perfect peace,
> Over all victorious,
> In its bright increase;
> Perfect, yet it floweth,
> Fuller ev'ry day;
> Perfect, yet it groweth,
> Deeper all the way.
> Stayed upon Jehovah,
> Hearts are fully blessed;
> Finding, as he promised,
> Perfect peace and rest.[2]

Perfect peace in the midst of severe physical pain—that's beyond our comprehension. It's a gift from God.

Peace among People

Scripture connects inner peace specifically to peace among people: "Let the peace that comes from Christ rule in your hearts. For as members of one body you are all called to live in peace" (Col. 3:15). If divine peace reigns within us, it should touch our most important relationships in family, among friends, and in church. But the peace of Christ affects an even broader set of human relationships than these.

Paul's letter to the Ephesians lays the spiritual foundation for peace among people. After showing that the death of Christ leads to our personal salvation (Eph. 2:4–10), Paul goes on to explore the corporate implications of the cross, focusing on the fundamental division between Jews and Gentiles:

For Christ himself has made peace between us Jews and you Gentiles by making us all one people. He has broken down the wall of hostility that used to separate us. By his death he ended the whole system of Jewish law that excluded the Gentiles. His purpose was to make peace between Jews and Gentiles by creating in himself one new person from the two groups. Together as one body, Christ reconciled both groups to God by means of his death, and our hostility toward each other was put to death.

Ephesians 2:14–16

The death of Jesus not only brings reconciliation between individuals and God but also creates reconciliation among people by destroying the hostility that keeps us from living peacefully together.

Sometimes we get so excited about the personal relevance of the cross that we neglect its corporate implications. We proclaim the possibility of peace with God and peace within ourselves without mentioning peace among people.

The tendency to neglect peace among people has pervaded Western Christian experience in the last few years because we have so often been shielded from human enemies. Christians who live in parts of the world where their faith in Christ can lead to persecution and even martyrdom are less inclined to forget about the human dimensions of divine peace. So are believers who live in countries ravaged by warfare, or in inner cities haunted by gang violence. Yet the tragic events of September 11, 2001, have awakened many of us from our naïve slumber. Now we feel vulnerable to an enemy who has openly stated his intention to kill as many Americans as possible. We ache with the thousands of people who lost loved ones in the devastating crashes and explosions of September 11. Thus, many of us find our prayers for peace to be broader than they have been before. We realize that peace with God and inner peace are wonderful but not adequate in a world filled with strife and misery. Along with believers throughout the world, we yearn for the fullness of divine peace.

God's peace offered through Christ entails reconciliation in all aspects of human society. Jesus Christ died on the cross and rose from the grave to restore peace to a broken world. Wherever there is conflict, whether inside individual hearts, or within families, or among brothers and sisters in church, or between different ethnic groups, or even between warring nations, Christ "wages peace" as his followers wield the paradoxical power of the cross.

The social dimensions of divine peace don't simply whitewash evil in a desperate attempt to "make nice." There are families, for example, that appear to be peaceful only because a powerful parent uses emotional violence to institute order. Churches sometimes pride themselves on their unity but avoid conflict only because the pastor silences open discussion. When we look for peace, we must keep before us the concept we find throughout Scripture. True peace will always include right relationships, justice for all persons, and wholeness in every dimension of life. Sometimes the path to true peace passes through strife before it arrives at its destination (Luke 12:52–53).

This means that no matter how much you enjoy peace with God and peace within your own heart, you must also pursue the corporate aspects of *shalom*—God has called you to be a peacemaker.

Becoming Peacemakers

Jesus said, "Blessed are the peacemakers, for they will be called children of God" (Matt. 5:9 NRSV). The rest of the New Testament echoes his exaltation of peacemaking. For example:

Let us therefore make every effort to do what leads to peace and to mutual edification.

Romans 14:19 NIV

Try to live in peace with everyone.

Hebrews 12:14

Both of these passages set peacemaking within the context of Christian community. We seek to live in peace as part of our *koinōnia* together.

Martin Luther is correct. The church of Jesus Christ is indeed a "mighty fortress," against which the gates of hell cannot prevail. But individual Christian communities are sometimes quite fragile. Frequently they shatter because members seek their own good rather than the benefit of the community as a whole. You and I are called to be peacemakers within our churches, to preserve the unity of Christian *koinōnia*.

To be a peacemaker in your church, you need, first, to "be completely humble and gentle" (Eph. 4:2 NIV). If you have a complaint or criticism, communicate it with humility, realizing that you could be wrong. In all interactions, treat people with gentleness, remembering that they are precious to God.

Second, be "patient with each other, making allowance for each other's faults because of your love" (Eph. 4:2). This call to patience implies that those around you will frustrate you with their slowness. They won't serve actively enough. They will pray too long or too little. Yet, you must put up with their faults (humbly and gently), even as they must put up with yours.

Third, if you are going to make peace within your church, you must "make every effort to keep the unity of the Spirit" (Eph. 4:3 NIV). Church unity is not something you can take for granted. Rather, you must seek it with vigorous effort. Where you see the beginning of division, snuff it out. If two church members are stuck in disagreement, help them reconcile. If something about the church begins to get on your nerves—and, believe me, something will—don't complain behind the leaders' backs or threaten to leave the church. Rather, talk directly and kindly with those who are responsible. Don't ever brandish the "I might leave" threat unless you're facing a major issue of intractable heresy or unrepentance. The tendency of American Christians to leave their churches over petty matters is one of the saddest and most unbiblical dimensions of church life in our society.

Fourth, peacemaking requires forgiveness. Over and over again, our Christian siblings will hurt us. If we hold on to the offense and the pain, if we fail to forgive or pretend to forgive without actually doing so, we will contribute to the demise of our Christian community just as much or more than the one who wronged us. When we do forgive, however, our relationships will be renewed and the body of Christ will be strengthened.

Everything I have said about peacemaking in church applies equally to family life. Humility, gentleness, patience, unity, and forgiveness belong at home. Unfortunately, home is often the toughest place to live out these virtues. When I come home from work after a day of exercising humility, gentleness, patience, and forgiveness with my staff and church members, I'm worn out. My children might get the last bit of peacemaking I can muster, though sometimes they don't even get the dregs. My wife, Linda, however, can get the brunt of my pride, insensitivity, impatience, and unforgiveness. If she's had a bad day too, you can imagine how little peace will bless our marriage that night.

As I grow in Christ, I'm learning to live out my faith at home first and foremost, not last and least. Because I'm human, as are my family members, forgiveness pervades our household. Without forgiveness, we'd soon build up walls of hostility that would damage our fellowship. That's the state of many families today, even Christian families. Husbands and wives have substituted pretending for peacemaking, thus storing up bitterness against one another. The same is often true of other family relationships. Only forgiveness modeled after God's own forgiveness and inspired by God's own Spirit will bring peace to our families.

Our peacemaking task begins right in front of us, in our closest relationships at home, at work, at school, and at church. But it doesn't stop there. As God's peacemakers, we must take the message and substance of peace into the whole world. How do we do this?

First, we announce the peacemaking work of Christ on the cross. Telling the good news about Jesus is essential to any Christian peacemaking effort. This good news invites others to renounce their sin and be reconciled to God. It opens the door so that they might begin to live in God's peace and join the ranks of divine peacemakers.

Second, we bring God's peace to the world by holding up the cross of Jesus as an example to emulate. Though the world might scoff at Christ's paradigm of self-sacrifice, it shows us all how to live.

Third, we extend divine peace into the world by living peaceably each day: "Do your part to live in peace with every-one, as much as possible" (Rom. 12:18). Notice that we are to live peaceably with "everyone," those inside of the church and those on the outside, those in our families and those at our workplace, the servers who forget to bring our food on time and the drivers who cut us off in the parking lot.

Fourth, we bring God's peace to the world by seeking his righteousness and justice. Jesus tells us to "seek first the king-dom [of God] and his righteousness" (Matt. 6:33 MDR). If we pursue divine righteousness in all of life, we will treat people with respect and dignity, especially those who are helpless and defenseless. We will make sure our practices and policies reflect God's revealed values, even when we operate in "the world." We won't turn the other way when we see injustice but will invest our energies so God's justice might take form in our world.

This last activity, doing justice in the world, has sparked considerable debate among Christians. When I was young, I watched Christians pummel one another verbally over American involvement in Vietnam. For some, a Christian commitment to peace demanded immediate withdrawal. For others, Christian values required that we free the Vietnamese from the domination of communism. In the 1980s, some Christian friends of mine protested the American nuclear arms buildup, even being arrested in acts of civil disobedience. Other Christian friends worked to help the United States make nuclear weapons, believing that their efforts furthered the cause of peace in the world.

Even though the relationship between Christian peacemaking and social activism can be confusing, we may not neglect it. Scripture calls us to make peace in every dimension of life and to seek justice in this world. Many peacemaking actions are clearly taught in Scripture and therefore require little debate. Building a home with Habitat for Humanity, sponsoring a child through World Vision, embracing someone from an ethnic background other than your own, caring for inmates through Prison Fellowship—all of these actions and countless more are clearly biblical. Let me urge you to invest yourself in doing that which God obviously favors, without spending all of your peacemaking efforts debating the difficult issues while doing nothing tangible.

When it comes to the tricky issues, however, we must seek God's wisdom in Scripture. Many advocates of social causes, including many Christians, do not ground their efforts in God's Word. Thus they easily go astray, either in goals or in strategies, and usually in both.

In a time of crisis and confusion, it is especially important for us to ground our social and political efforts on the solid foundation of Scripture. In the days since the terrorist attacks on America, some well-intentioned Christians have said things in anger without weighing their words on the scale of God's Word. One caller to a Christian talk show called for the obliteration of the whole nation of Afghanistan. Many others, in talking about Osama bin Laden and the Taliban, have forgotten the call of Jesus to love our enemies. Their rhetoric has gone far beyond a biblical call for justice, indulging an understandable but unbiblical desire for revenge. It's much harder to follow Jesus' command to love our enemies when we have real enemies, isn't it?

Most of us will not be in a position to decide what kinds of military activity are appropriate for the United States to take in response to terrorism. Thus we will not be in the tricky position of evaluating American interests from a Christian perspective. But all of us are called to pray for our leaders, including those who wield such immense military authority (1 Tim. 2:2). Many of these leaders are brothers and sisters in Christ who need divine wisdom now more than ever. As peacemakers, we must pray for them and for all who exercise leadership over the nations, no matter what their faith commitments. Yet, as we pray, we must also remember the challenging words of Jesus, "But I say, love your enemies! Pray for those who persecute you!" (Matt. 5:44). Pray for Osama bin Laden? Pray for those who would seek to kill innocent Americans? That's exactly what peacemaking in the mode of Jesus requires.

As we pray for peace in our world, let us not forget to be peacemakers right where we live. When I consider Jesus' blessing of peacemakers, I think of a ministry in Hollywood, California, called City Dwellers. In my last years at Hollywood Presbyterian, I was privileged to watch this ministry grow. Members of the City Dwellers team live in one of the neighborhoods in Hollywood, a barrio filled primarily with lower class immigrant families. Violence, crime, poverty, and injustice are common in "the neighborhood." City Dwellers seek God's *shalom* for that community (Jer. 29:7).

City Dweller teammates are usually young adults who spend a year living in Hollywood as peacemakers. Their ministry is multifaceted. They share the gospel and their possessions with their neighbors. They shepherd children and encourage parents. They seek justice for people whose ignorance of American society makes them easy targets for oppressors. They feed the hungry and visit prisoners in jail. They comfort parents whose children are shot in drive-by shootings. They teach young people academic skills and they teach them about Jesus.

The Peace That Lies Ahead

When City Dwellers share their lives with Hispanic kids or when World Vision mobilizes the church to care for victims of famine, you catch a glimpse of the peace that lies ahead. When a family moves into its very first home, one that was built by volunteers with Habitat for Humanity, or when men at a Promise Keepers' gathering cast off their racism and embrace other men whose skin isn't the same color as their own, you can see the dawning of the future. When a husband and wife choose forgiveness over bitterness, or a person of power chooses the way of humility rather than harshness, you taste a morsel of the messianic banquet yet to come. When people whose lives have been imprisoned by brokenness find wholeness and freedom through Christ, you peek through a window into eternity. Every time God's peace invades our present existence, we get a foretaste of the infinitely greater peace that will someday envelop heaven and earth.

The last Book of the Bible, the Revelation of John, reveals a future filled with divine peace:

> Then I saw a new heaven and a new earth, for the old heaven and the old earth had disappeared. And the sea was also gone. And I saw the holy city, the new Jerusalem, coming down from God out of heaven like a beautiful bride prepared for her husband. I heard a loud shout from the throne, saying, "Look, the home of God is now among his people! He will live with them, and they will be his people. God himself will be with them. He will remove all of their sorrows, and there will be no more death or sorrow or crying or pain. For the old world and its evils are gone forever."
>
> Revelation 21:1–4

God will not obliterate his creation but renew it to match his original intention. The work of reconciliation will be completed, and we will live with God, just as we were supposed to from the beginning. *Koinōnia,* lost in the fall, regained in the cross, will be fully restored.

Christians are people who live now in intimate fellowship with God and with God's people. In these relationships we experience genuine peace, yet not the fullness of peace. By the indwelling Spirit, we step into the future, enjoying peace with God and all its benefits, but only in part. We walk intimately with God, though sin keeps nipping at our heels. We share life with our Christian brothers and sisters, sometimes loving one another as Christ has loved us and sometimes clobbering one another like a bunch of squabbling siblings.

We can see heaven beginning to arise on the horizon, but the dawn tarries.

The biblical vision of the peace that lies ahead helps draw us near to God. It enables us to trust him in the midst of a world filled with brokenness and strife. This vision also motivates us to be peacemakers, even when our notions of peace and our approaches to peacemaking seem naive to a jaded world. Finally, the biblical picture of peace yet to come binds us together with other Christians in a *koinōnia* of hope.

> May the God of hope fill you with all joy and peace as you trust in him, so that you may overflow with hope by the power of the Holy Spirit.
>
> Romans 15:13 NIV

PRACTICAL QUESTIONS AND ANSWERS

1. "For a lot of personal reasons, the peace of God seems far removed from my daily life right now. How can I really know divine peace each day?"

> *Peace is a gift from God. Every individual experience of peace rests on the peacemaking work of Christ on the cross. If you are lacking peace, don't try to make yourself feel peaceful. Rather, turn to the Lord. Cry out to him for help. Spend time with him on a regular basis. I am always impressed by how much more peacefully I take on the problems of the day when I have begun that day with Christ.*
>
> *The more you focus your mind on God and the things of God, the more you will dwell in his peace. This theme appears throughout the Scripture. Isaiah says to the Lord, "You will keep in perfect peace all who trust in you, whose thoughts are fixed on you!" (Isa. 26:3 NLT). If you are struggling with doubt or worry, I'll bet that your mind is focused somewhere else, probably on yourself and your problems. Ask God for the grace to set your mind on him.*

Our individual experience of God's peace depends, largely, on our participation in the community of God's people. When we struggle with all those feelings that squelch God's peace within us, our brothers and sisters in Christ will listen to us, pray for us, and encourage us. If you want to know God's peace each day, make sure you don't seek it alone.

2. "There are so many ways to be involved in God's peacemaking work that I feel overwhelmed. I don't even know where to start. What should I do to begin living as a peacemaker?"

First, look at what is right in front of you. Chances are that you'll find numerous opportunities to be a peacemaker right in your home, classroom, office, neighborhood, or church. Second, ask God for direction concerning which ministry of peacemaking to invest in. Beware of the tendency to get over-involved. Third, what is your passion? Often God directs us through our convictions and strong feelings. Fourth, always seek God's will through studying and meditating on Scripture. You will hear the Spirit's voice as you reflect on what the Spirit has already said in the Bible. Fifth, allow your Christian community to help you discern where to invest your energies as a member of God's peacemaking team. When your brothers and sisters listen to you and pray with you for guidance, they'll also help you distinguish between God's call and your own enthusiasm.

Notes

Preface

1. The woman in this story was not actually named "Lisa," though the details of the story are otherwise accurate. All of the personal stories in this book are true. Sometimes I use people's actual names. Sometimes I change names to protect people's privacy. At all times I try hard to be accurate in all that I relate.

Chapter 1: *What Is the Christian Life?*

1. When well-known English translations of the Bible are not accurate enough for the purposes of this book, I will supply my own translation, noted by my initials MDR.

2. Henry Liddell and Robert Scott, revised by Henry Jones, *A Greek-English Lexicon* (Oxford: Clarendon Press, 1968), 970.

3. C. S. Lewis, *The Great Divorce* (New York: Touchstone, 1996), 13–26.

Chapter 3: *Intimate Fellowship in the Body of Christ*

1. Wade Clark Roof, *A Generation of Seekers* (San Francisco: HarperSanFrancisco, 1993), 256.

2. Livy, *The Rise of Rome*, 2.32.9–12.

Chapter 5: *Intimate Fellowship and Prayer*

1. "Why We Pray," *LIFE*, March 1994, 54ff.

2. Peter Jaret, "Can Prayer Heal?" *Health*, March 1998, 48ff; "Good News on Prayer," *Time*, August 24, 1998, 86.

3. "Why We Pray," 60.

Chapter 6: *Intimate Fellowship and Spiritual Guidance*

1. Anita Baskin, "The Spirit of Barbie," *Omni*, March 1994, 76ff.

Chapter 7: *Intimate Fellowship and Worship*

1. John Calvin, *Institutes*, 3.20.31.

Chapter 8: *Intimate Fellowship and the World*

1. Stephen L. Carter, *The Culture of Disbelief* (New York: Basic Books, 1993).

Chapter 9: *Intimate Fellowship and Our Mission in the World*

1. For a thorough treatment of the church as "missional," see Darrell Guder, ed., *The Missional Church* (Grand Rapids: Eerdmans, 1998) and Craig Van Gelder, *The Essence of the Church* (Grand Rapids: Baker, 2000).

2. For more on William Wilberforce, see "The 'Shrimp' Who Stopped Slavery," by Christopher D. Hancock, in *Christian History,* Issue 53, 1997, 12–19.

Chapter 10: *Intimate Fellowship and Transformed Living*

1. *Westminster Confession of Faith,* 13:2. Italics added.

2. Jonathan Swift, *Gulliver's Travels,* Part 4 (1726).

3. Martin Luther, *Preface to the Letter of St. Paul to the Romans,* trans. Andrew Thornton, OSB, retrieved from Books for the Ages, AGES Software, Version 1.0, © 1997, 15.

Chapter 11: *Intimate Fellowship and Love*

1. *What is Love?* by Howard Jones, Live Acoustic America, Plump Records.

2. The idea of the "prodigal father" was first suggested to me through the writing of Helmut Thielicke, *The Waiting Father: Sermons on the Parables of Jesus,* trans. John Doberstein (New York: Harper, 1959).

Chapter 12: *Intimate Fellowship and Peace*

1. "The Life of the Rev. John Wesley," in *The Works of John Wesley,* 3d ed., vol. 5 (1872). Retrieved through Ages Software.

2. Words to *Like a River Glorious* are in the public domain. For more on the life of Frances Havergal, see Jane Stuart Smith and Betty Carlson, *Great Christian Hymn Writers* (Wheaton: Crossway Books, 1997), 79–84.

Mark D. Roberts is senior pastor of Irvine Presbyterian Church in Southern California and teaches courses in New Testament at Fuller Theological Seminary. Previously, he served on the pastoral staff of Hollywood Presbyterian Church with Lloyd Ogilvie. He has an earned A.B., M.A., and Ph.D. from Harvard. The author of *Ezra, Nehemiah, Esther* in the Communicator's Commentary Series, Mark lives with his wife, Linda, and two children in Irvine, California.